Grades 4–8

NotebookReference

Science Fact Book

Second Edition

AMERICAN
EDUCATION
PUBLISHING™

An imprint of Carson-Dellosa Publishing
Greensboro, North Carolina

American Education Publishing™
An imprint of Carson-Dellosa Publishing LLC
P.O. Box 35665
Greensboro, NC 27425 USA

Printed inthe USA • All rights reserved.   ISBN 978-0-7696-4346-5

05-209148091

Table of Contents

Table of Contents

LIFE SCIENCE

Plants and Photosynthesis

Plants

Green, flowering plants grow all around you. Beautiful red roses, tall cornstalks, or prickly thistle weeds are all green, flowering plants. Green, flowering plants have six parts: **stem**, **root**, **leaf**, **flower**, **fruit,** and **seeds**.

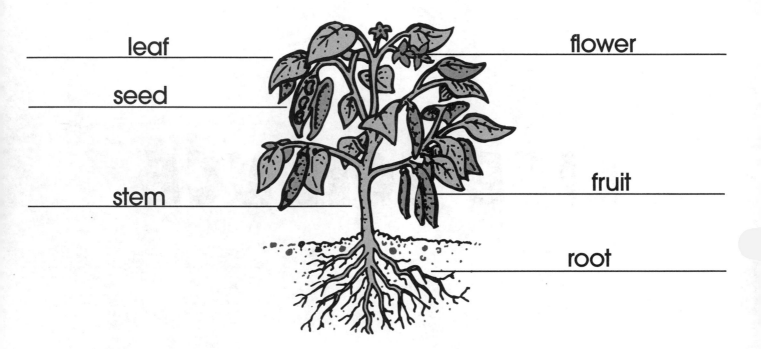

leaf

seed

stem

flower

fruit

root

Photosynthesis

Leaves work like little factories making food for the plant, using a green material called **chlorophyll**. In each leaf, chlorophyll is like a little "green machine," changing water and air into food. Like most machines, chlorophyll needs energy to work. The green machine gets its energy from sunlight. This process is called **photosynthesis**. Without sunlight, the leaves could not make food.

Flowers and Pollination

Flowers have a very important job. Most plants produce seeds inside the flower that will become new flowering plants.

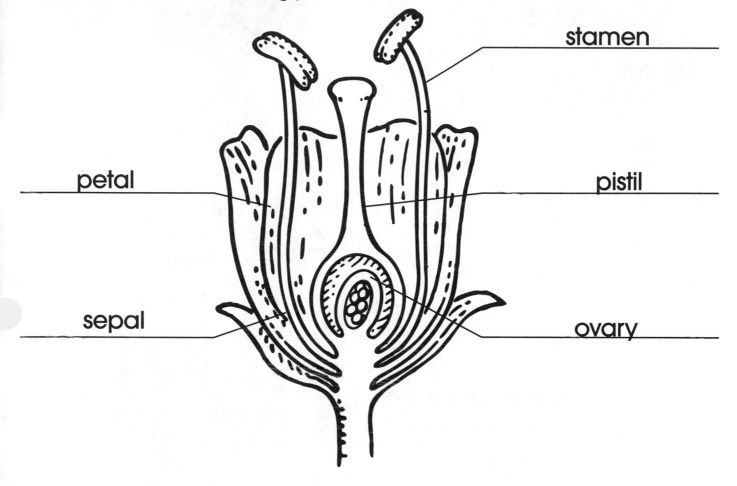

stamen

petal

pistil

sepal

ovary

Bees, butterflies, other insects, and hummingbirds help flowers reproduce by carrying pollen from one flower to another. This process is called **pollination**. The pollen grains travel down through the style into the ovary of the flower. The pollen grains fertilize the egg cells in the ovules, and seeds begin to form. Later, as the seeds grow, the ovary walls grow into the fruit that will house the seeds.

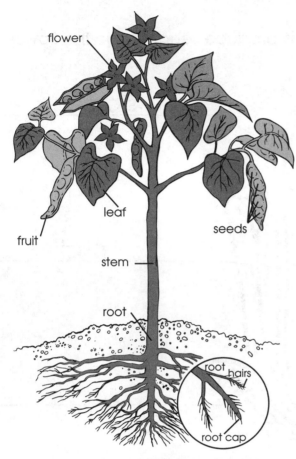

flower

leaf

fruit

seeds

stem

root

root hairs

root cap

Outer Parts of a Flower

petals

sepals

receptacle

Reproductive Parts of a Flower

Pistil—The pistil is the female reproductive organ of a flower. It is composed of three parts: stigma, style, and ovary.

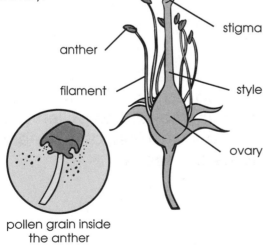

anther

filament

stigma

style

ovary

pollen grain inside the anther

Stamen—The stamen is the male reproductive organ of a flower. It is composed of two parts: anther and filament.

Seeds

(corn seed)
Monocot—A monocot has only one cotyledon, or seedleaf. The embryo's food is stored in the endosperm.

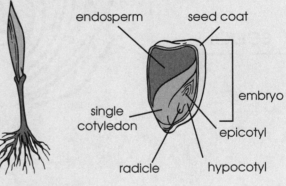

endosperm

seed coat

single cotyledon

embryo

radicle

epicotyl

hypocotyl

**monocot seedling
(one leaf)**

(bean seed)
Dicot—A dicot has two cotyledons, or seedleaves. The embryo's food is stored in the two cotyledons.

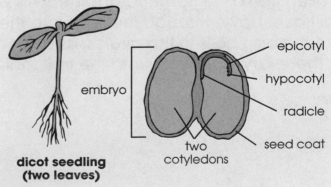

embryo

epicotyl

hypocotyl

radicle

seed coat

two cotyledons

**dicot seedling
(two leaves)**

Plant Systems

Soil

Soil does more than just make your hands dirty. It is important for making plants grow.

Soil is made of **rock**, **humus**, **air,** and **water**. The rock is often in the form of sand or clay. Sand is easy to dig, but it doesn't hold water. Clay holds water, but is packed too tightly to let plants grow. Humus is matter that was once alive, but now it is decayed or rotted. Humus gives nutrients to the soil. Plants need nutrients to grow.

Root System

The plant's root system pulls water and minerals from the ground. There are two kinds of root systems. Some plants have one main root that grows deep into the ground. This is called a **tap** root. Other plants have shallow roots with many branches. These roots are called **fibrous** roots. Attached to both root systems are tiny root **hairs** that do all the work of absorbing water.

Monocot and Dicot Plants

Monocot and Dicot Plants

How does the plant get its food? Thin tubes in the stem carry food from the leaf to the rest of the plant. Other tubes carry water and minerals from the roots to the leaves. Both kinds of tubes are found in bundles in the stem.

The tube bundles are arranged in two ways. A **monocot** plant has bundles scattered throughout the stem. A **dicot** plant has bundles arranged in a ring around the edge of the stem.

Monocot   **Dicot**

Parts of a Seed

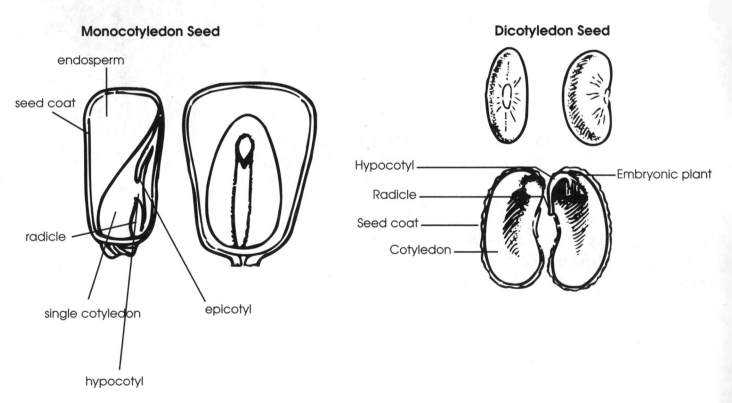

Monocotyledon Seed

endosperm

seed coat

radicle

single cotyledon

epicotyl

hypocotyl

Dicotyledon Seed

Hypocotyl ——————— Embryonic plant

Radicle ———

Seed coat ———

Cotyledon ———

Tree Parts

All trees have many of the same parts as the plants that grow in your garden— only much larger.

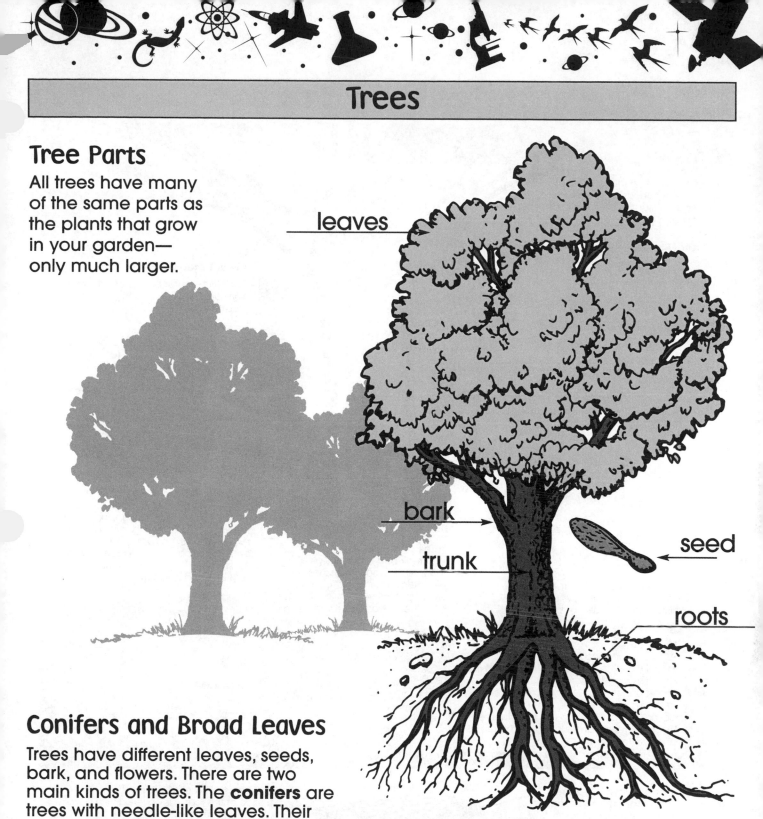

leaves

bark

trunk

seed

roots

Conifers and Broad Leaves

Trees have different leaves, seeds, bark, and flowers. There are two main kinds of trees. The **conifers** are trees with needle-like leaves. Their seeds are found in cones. Conifers stay green all year long. The **broad-leaved** trees have leaves of different sizes and shapes. Broad-leaved trees often lose their leaves in the fall. In warm regions, some broad-leaved trees keep their leaves all year long.

Parts of a Tree

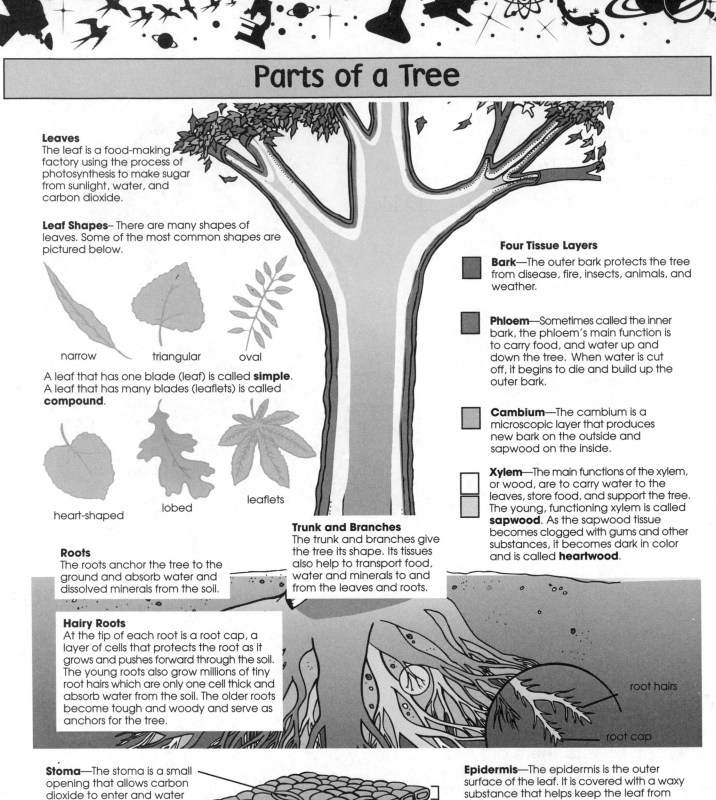

Leaves
The leaf is a food-making factory using the process of photosynthesis to make sugar from sunlight, water, and carbon dioxide.

Leaf Shapes– There are many shapes of leaves. Some of the most common shapes are pictured below.

narrow

triangular

oval

A leaf that has one blade (leaf) is called **simple**. A leaf that has many blades (leaflets) is called **compound**.

heart-shaped

lobed

leaflets

Roots
The roots anchor the tree to the ground and absorb water and dissolved minerals from the soil.

Hairy Roots
At the tip of each root is a root cap, a layer of cells that protects the root as it grows and pushes forward through the soil. The young roots also grow millions of tiny root hairs which are only one cell thick and absorb water from the soil. The older roots become tough and woody and serve as anchors for the tree.

Trunk and Branches
The trunk and branches give the tree its shape. Its tissues also help to transport food, water and minerals to and from the leaves and roots.

Four Tissue Layers

Bark—The outer bark protects the tree from disease, fire, insects, animals, and weather.

Phloem—Sometimes called the inner bark, the phloem's main function is to carry food, and water up and down the tree. When water is cut off, it begins to die and build up the outer bark.

Cambium—The cambium is a microscopic layer that produces new bark on the outside and sapwood on the inside.

Xylem—The main functions of the xylem, or wood, are to carry water to the leaves, store food, and support the tree. The young, functioning xylem is called **sapwood**. As the sapwood tissue becomes clogged with gums and other substances, it becomes dark in color and is called **heartwood**.

root hairs

root cap

Stoma—The stoma is a small opening that allows carbon dioxide to enter and water vapor to exit the leaf.

Chloroplasts—Chloroplasts are small green bodies containing the pigment chlorophyll. They are found floating within the palisade and spongy cells.

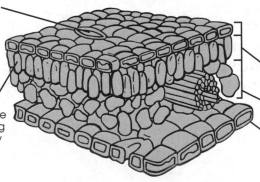

Epidermis—The epidermis is the outer surface of the leaf. It is covered with a waxy substance that helps keep the leaf from drying out.

Palisade Layer—The spongy and palisade cells are the food-making cells.

spongy layer

vein

How a Tree Grows

Trees Grow Taller

The end of each twig has a terminal bud with special cells that divide and make the twig grow longer. Each year's growth comes from a bud that contains the beginnings of a twig, leaves, and flowers.

Inside a Bud

bud scales

immature leaves

immature stem

Scale leaves cover and protect young flowers, leaves, and stems inside the bud.

lateral bud

leaf bud

leaf scar

One-year-old side shoot formed by a lateral bud.

Terminal Bud
The terminal (leading) bud is protected from weather by thick, overlapping scales.

Terminal buds produce a hormone called *auxin* that prevents the growth of lateral buds. If the terminal bud dies or is removed, the lateral bud develops.

Last Year's Growth
Last year's growth extends from the terminal bud back to the scale scar.

Scale Scar
The scale scar, or growth rings, consists of lines around the twig that show where last year's terminal bud was located.

Increase in Growth
The neighboring trees were cut down or damaged, perhaps by a storm or disease. Thus, the tree has received more sunlight.

Growth Begins

Slow Growth
There is competition with neighboring trees for sunlight.

"V" Marking
This marking indicates that a branch grew at this point.

Decrease in Growth
This is probably due to drought or insects.

Normal Growth

Medullary Ray
This carries nutrients inward toward the center of the tree.

heartwood

sapwood

Heartwood
This helps to support the tree.

Sapwood
This carries water from the roots to the leaves.

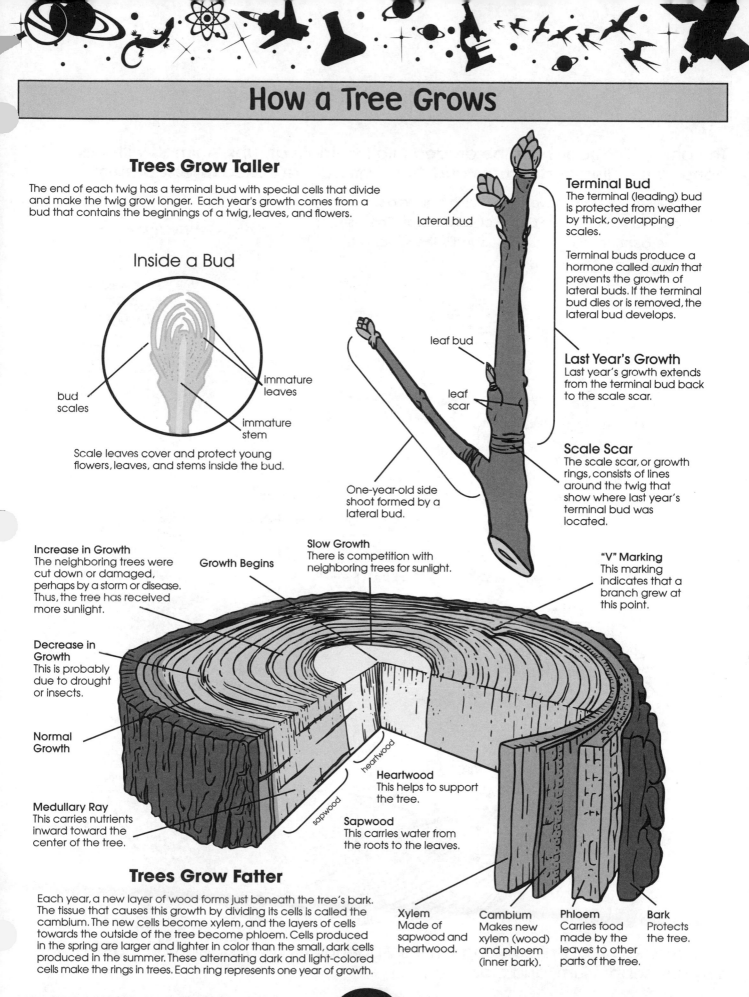

Trees Grow Fatter

Each year, a new layer of wood forms just beneath the tree's bark. The tissue that causes this growth by dividing its cells is called the cambium. The new cells become xylem, and the layers of cells towards the outside of the tree become phloem. Cells produced in the spring are larger and lighter in color than the small, dark cells produced in the summer. These alternating dark and light-colored cells make the rings in trees. Each ring represents one year of growth.

Xylem
Made of sapwood and heartwood.

Cambium
Makes new xylem (wood) and phloem (inner bark).

Phloem
Carries food made by the leaves to other parts of the tree.

Bark
Protects the tree.

The Animal Kingdom

The animal kingdom can be divided into two main groups. Animals with back-bones are called **vertebrates** and those without are called **invertebrates**.

It's All in the Name! Every living thing is given a scientific name made from two Greek or Latin words. The first is the *genus* name, and the second is the *species*.

human = *Homo sapiens*
dog = *Canis familiaris*
cat = *Felis domesticus*

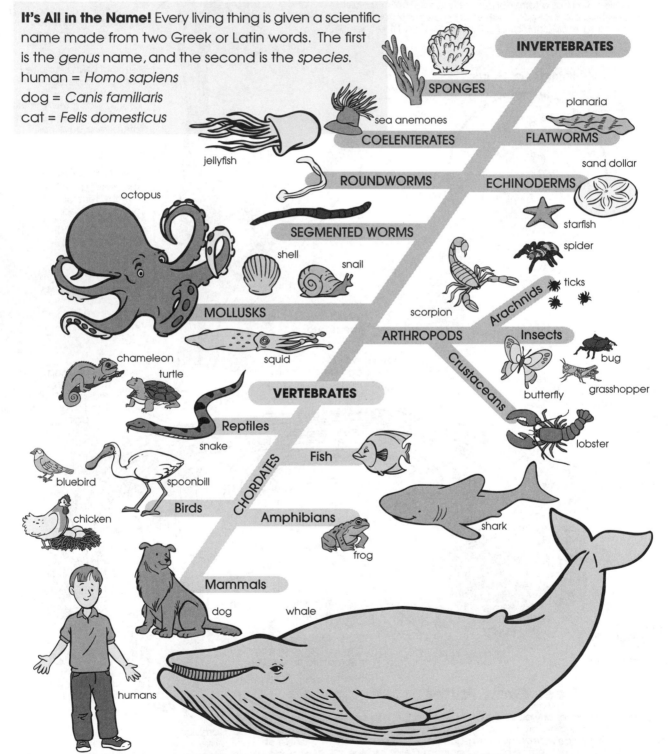

A Classification of Animals chart in the Appendices breaks down animals by phylum, subphylum, and class.

Invertebrates

Some animals do not have backbones. These animals are called **invertebrates**. Worms, centipedes, and insects are all invertebrates.

There are many more invertebrates than vertebrates. Nine out of ten animals are invertebrates.

Insects

The largest group of animals belongs to the group called **invertebrates**—or animals without backbones. This large group is the **insect** group.

Insects are easy to tell apart from other animals. Adult insects have three body parts and six legs. The first body part is the **head**. On the head are the mouth, eyes and antennae. The second body part is the **thorax**. On it are the legs and wings. The third part is the **abdomen**. On it are small openings for breathing.

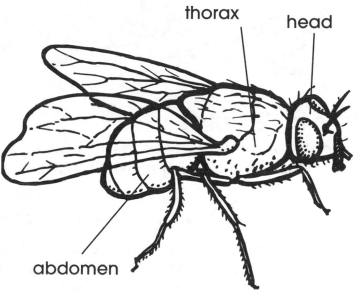

thorax   head

abdomen

Butterflies vs. Moths

People sometimes confuse butterflies with moths, but there are some important differences.

Butterflies . . .

- fly by day.
- have antennae with "knobs."
- have thin, hairless bodies.
- rest with their wings held upright.

Moths . . .

- fly at night.
- have antennae without "knobs."
- have plump, furry bodies.
- rest with their wings spread out flat.

Vertebrates

Which part of your body helps you stand tall or sit up straight? It is your backbone. You are a member of a large group of animals that all have backbones. Animals with backbones are called **vertebrates**. Birds, fish, reptiles, amphibians, and mammals are all vertebrates.

Special Features

Have you ever tried to see a fawn standing silently in a forest? You have to look very closely. Its coloring makes it hard to see. This is called **camouflage**.

Some animals use camouflage to protect themselves from their enemies. Other animals use their strength or speed for protection.

The octopus and the squid have a special defense weapon. They squirt out a special inky chemical when threatened. This chemical acts like a smoke screen and also dulls the senses of their enemies.

Endangered Animals

You will never see a dodo bird or a saber-tooth tiger. These animals are gone forever. They are **extinct**.

Animals in danger of becoming extinct are **endangered**. There may not be enough of them to reproduce.

Hibernation

Have you ever wondered why some animals hibernate? Some animals sleep all winter. This sleep is called **hibernation**.

Animals get their warmth and energy from food. Some animals cannot find enough food in the winter. They must eat large amounts of food in the autumn. Their bodies store this food as fat. Then, in winter, they hibernate. Their bodies live on the stored fat. Since their bodies need much less food during hibernation, they can stay alive without eating anymore food during the winter.

Some animals that hibernate are bats, chipmunks, bears, snakes, and turtles.

Food Chains

Food Chain

Did you ever wonder where the food you eat comes from? The hamburger you eat comes from a cow. The cow eats the green grass in the pasture. The cow eats the grass and you eat the cow. This is a **food chain**. It can be written like this:

$$\text{grass} \longrightarrow \text{cow} \longrightarrow \text{person}$$

Each arrow between an animal and its food is called a **strand**.

Producers and Consumers

Producers are organisms, such as green plants, that use light energy to make food from carbon dioxide and water in the presence of chlorophyll. Consumers are organisms, such as animals, that are unable to make their own food and must obtain food from other organisms.

Food Group Pyramid

In order to stay healthy, you should follow the rules stated in the food group pyramid.

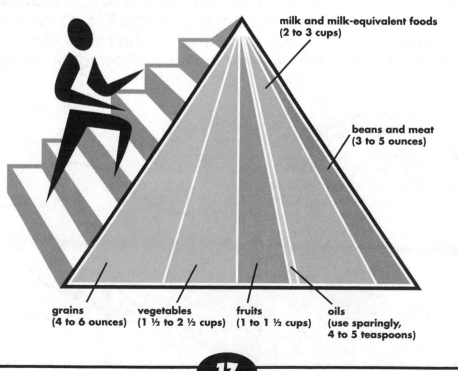

milk and milk-equivalent foods
(2 to 3 cups)

beans and meat
(3 to 5 ounces)

grains
(4 to 6 ounces)

vegetables
(1 ½ to 2 ½ cups)

fruits
(1 to 1 ½ cups)

oils
(use sparingly,
4 to 5 teaspoons)

Food Webs

Food Chains in the Sea

All living things in the seas also depend on each other for food. The food chain begins with sea plants called **phytoplankton**. A huge variety of tiny animals called **zooplankton** feed on the phytoplankton. These animals include shrimp, copepods and jellyfish. Some of the most common fish—herring, anchovies and sprats—feed on zooplankton. These fish are eaten by others, such as tuna and mackerel, which in turn are eaten by the superpredators, such as sharks and dolphins. This pattern of eating is called a **food chain**.

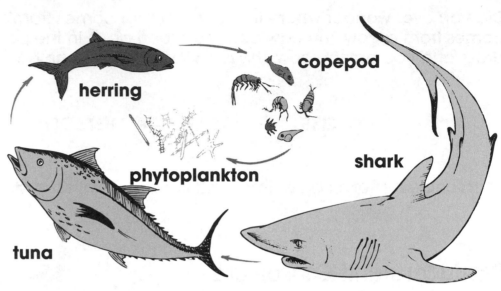

Prairie Food Web

In complex grassland communities like the prairie, the flow of food and energy cannot be described by a simple food chain. Instead, it is represented by a series of interconnected food chains called a **food web**. The many kinds of producers and consumers in the prairie community provide a wide variety of food sources.

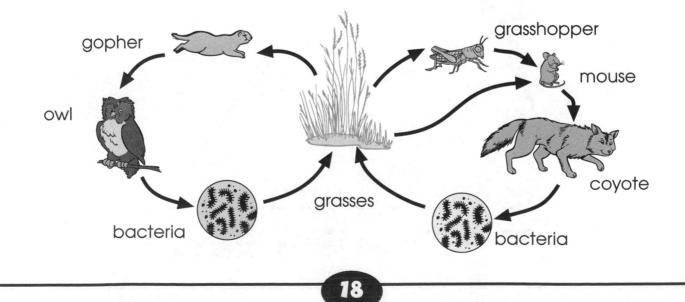

Vertebrates

Vertebrates are animals with a backbone. Most vertebrates have a bony backbone, called a **spinal column**. The spinal column is made of bones called **vertebrae**.

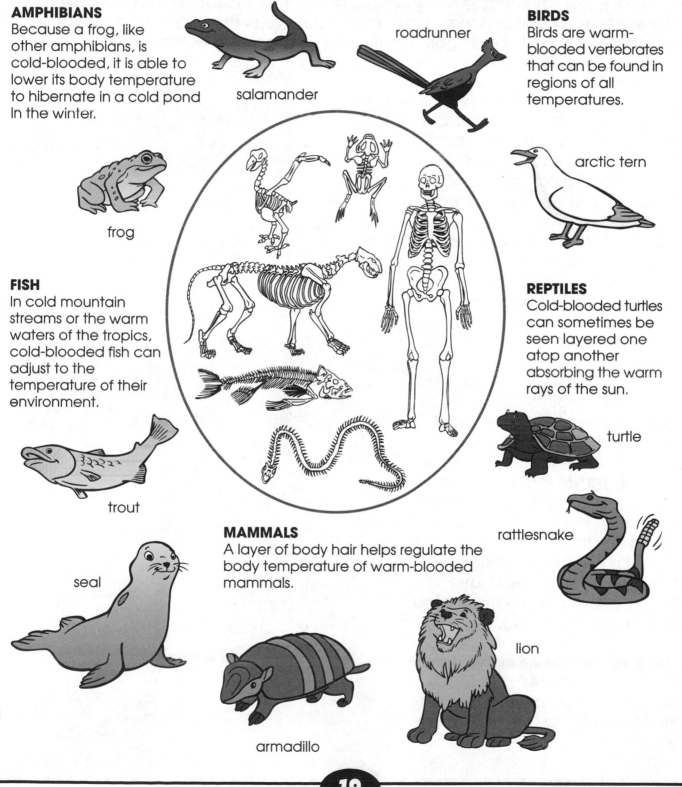

AMPHIBIANS

Because a frog, like other amphibians, is cold-blooded, it is able to lower its body temperature to hibernate in a cold pond In the winter.

salamander

roadrunner

BIRDS

Birds are warm-blooded vertebrates that can be found in regions of all temperatures.

frog

arctic tern

FISH

In cold mountain streams or the warm waters of the tropics, cold-blooded fish can adjust to the temperature of their environment.

REPTILES

Cold-blooded turtles can sometimes be seen layered one atop another absorbing the warm rays of the sun.

turtle

trout

rattlesnake

MAMMALS

A layer of body hair helps regulate the body temperature of warm-blooded mammals.

seal

lion

armadillo

Skeletal System

A **system** is a group of body organs that together perform one or more vital functions. Humans have a skeletal system, a nervous system, an integumentary system, a circulatory system, a digestive system, a respiratory system, a nervous system, a urinary system, an endocrine system, a reproductive system, and a muscular system. All these systems work together efficiently in a healthy human being.

The skeletal system has about 206 bones. These bones support the body and give it shape, protect internal organs (such as the brain, spinal cord, and heart), and work with muscles to provide movement. The bones store minerals, releasing them to the bloodstream as needed, and have soft, spongy, jellylike centers called **bone marrow**. Yellow marrow is mainly stored fat; red marrow produces red blood cells.

Two or more bones come together at a joint. Fixed joints, like those of the skull, are permanently fused together. Movable joints are held together by strong, flexible tissues called **ligaments** that allow for a variety of movement. For example, the hips and shoulders have ball-and-socket joints which allow for rotational movement, while the elbows, fingers, and toes have hinge joints that limit movement to bending and extending.

The smallest bones lie in the ears: the malleus (hammer), the incus (anvil), and the stapes (stirrup). The longest bone is the femur, or thighbone.

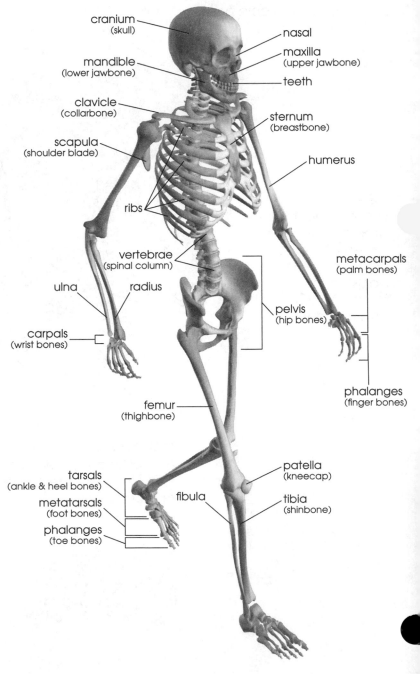

cranium (skull)
nasal
mandible (lower jawbone)
maxilla (upper jawbone)
teeth
clavicle (collarbone)
sternum (breastbone)
scapula (shoulder blade)
humerus
ribs
vertebrae (spinal column)
metacarpals (palm bones)
ulna
radius
pelvis (hip bones)
carpals (wrist bones)
phalanges (finger bones)
femur (thighbone)
patella (kneecap)
tarsals (ankle & heel bones)
fibula
tibia (shinbone)
metatarsals (foot bones)
phalanges (toe bones)

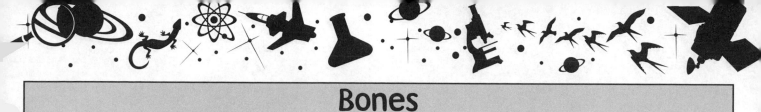
Your skeleton helps your body move. It does this by giving your **muscles** a place to attach. Your skeleton also protects the soft organs inside your body from injury.

Bones have a hard, outer layer made of **calcium**. Inside each bone is a soft, spongy layer that looks like a honeycomb. The hollow spaces in the honeycomb are filled with marrow. Every minute, millions of blood cells die. But you don't need to worry. The bone marrow works like a little factory, making new blood cells for you.

Bone Parts

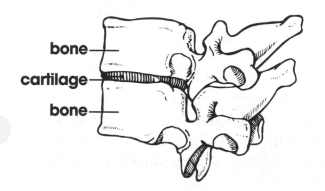

When you were born, your skeleton was made of soft bones called **cartilage**. As you grew, most of that cartilage turned into bone. However, all people still have some cartilage in their bodies. Our noses and our ears are cartilage, and there are pads of cartilage between sections of our back-bone that act as cushions.

Besides supporting the body, the bones also serve other important purposes. They are storage houses for important minerals like calcium and phosphorous. The center of the bone, called **bone marrow**, produces new blood cells for our bodies.

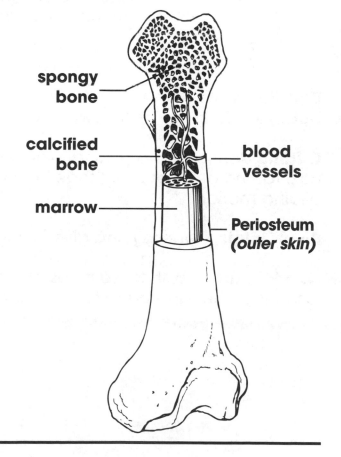

Joints

The place two bones meet is called a **joint**. Joints allow us to bend, twist, and turn our bodies. The human body has several different types of joints. Each allows a different kind of movement.

Hinge Joints — These joints can only move in one direction, like a door hinge. One bone works against another. Movement is back and forth on one plane.

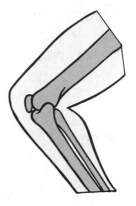

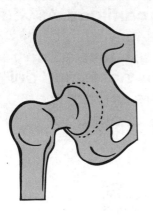

Ball-and-Socket Joints — These joints provide us with swinging and rotating movements. Make a fist with one hand. Cup the fingers of the other. Put your fist inside the cupped hand. You can turn your fist (the ball) in any direction within your cupped hand (the socket).

Saddle Joints — These joints move in two directions, back and forth, up and down or in rotation.

Gliding Joints — In a gliding joint, several bones next to one another bend together in limited gliding motion.

Pivot Joints — These joints give us a rotating motion.

Fixed Joints — With these types of joints, bones are fused together and permit no movement.

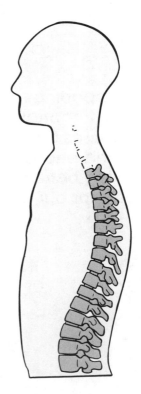

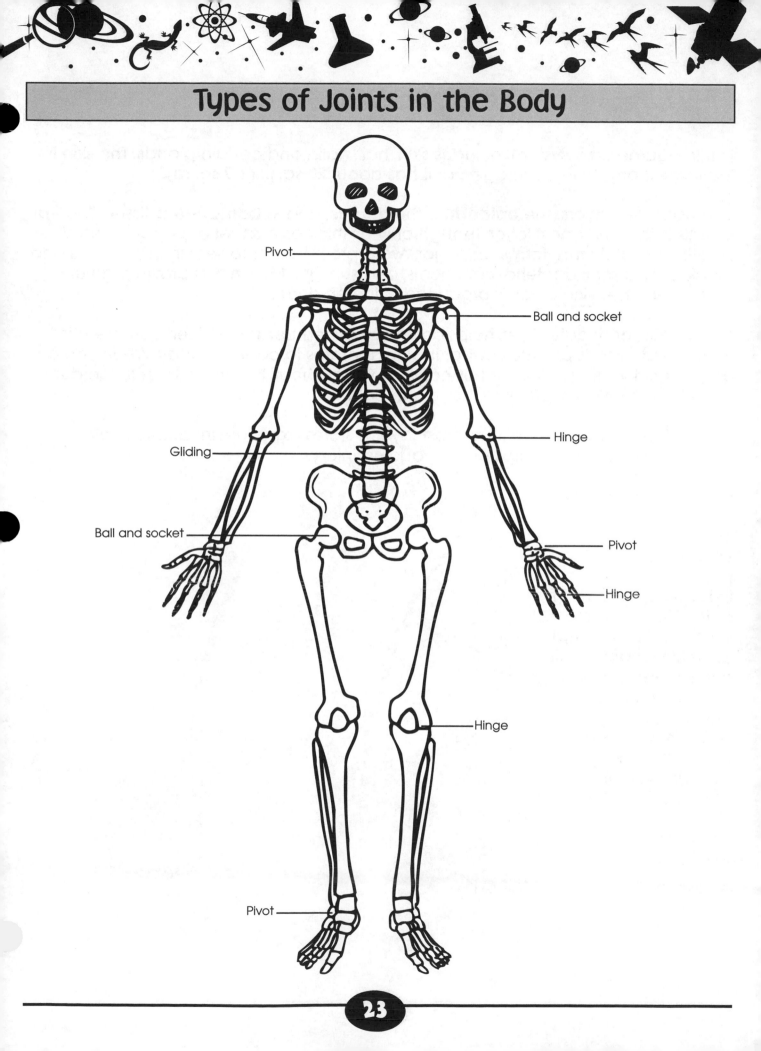

Pivot

Ball and socket

Hinge

Gliding

Ball and socket

Pivot

Hinge

Hinge

Pivot

Integumentary System

The integumentary system includes skin, hair, nails, and certain glands. The skin is the largest organ; the average adult has about 20 sq. ft. (1.9 sq. m).

Skin has three layers: the **epidermis**, the **dermis**, and **subcutaneous** tissue. The epidermis is the outermost layer. Though only as thick as a sheet of paper, it contains keratin, a protein that forms an almost waterproof barrier to seal in tissue fluids and block out harmful bacteria, chemicals, and sunlight. Melanin, a brown pigment that determines skin color, is produced in the epidermis.

The dermis, or middle layer, helps control body temperature. When you are hot, your sweat glands produce sweat that evaporates to cool the body. When you are cold, blood vessels in the dermis narrow to retain heat. Nerve endings in the dermis let you feel pain, pressure, heat, and cold.

Subcutaneous tissue is the innermost layer. It stores extra fuel in fat cells, helps retain body heat, and helps protect against injury.

Hair contains keratin and is mostly nonliving; only the bulb, where hair growth begins, is alive. Sebaceous glands in hair follicles secrete an oil that makes hair and skin smooth. Hair color is also determined by melanin.

Nails are layers of flat, dead, keratin-containing cells.

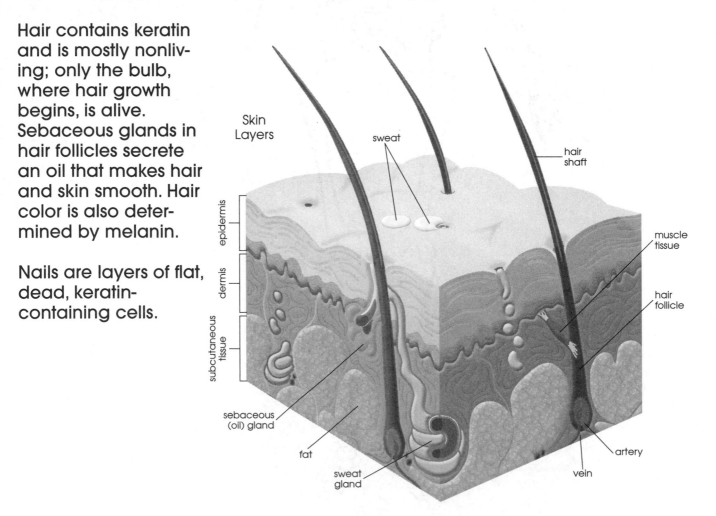

Skin Layers

sweat

hair shaft

epidermis

dermis

subcutaneous tissue

muscle tissue

hair follicle

sebaceous (oil) gland

fat

sweat gland

vein

artery

Muscular System

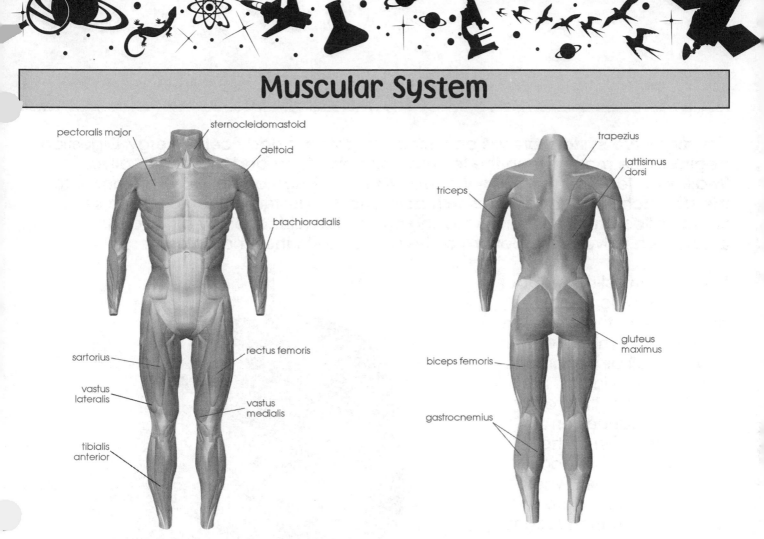

Muscles hold our skeletons together, give our bodies shape, and help us move. Muscles account for about half of our body weight and, because they warm when used, they supply about 80% of our body's heat.

Muscles are made up of threadlike cells bound together to form muscle fibers. A muscle group, like a biceps, contains bundles of these muscle fibers. Our bodies have three kinds of muscles: **skeletal**, **smooth**, and **cardiac**.

Skeletal muscles attach to bones by tendons and move bones by pulling, not pushing. Skeletal muscles work as pairs (e.g., your biceps raises your forearm while your triceps lowers it) or as larger groups (e.g., you use about 17 muscles to smile).

Skeletal muscles are called "voluntary" muscles because you choose when to use them. However, skeletal muscles may also react involuntarily (e.g., to pull your hand away from a hot object). Skeletal muscles tire when used for long periods of time. Our bodies have about 660 skeletal muscles. Smooth muscle is found in most internal organs. Cardiac muscle is found only in the heart. Both smooth and cardiac muscles work involuntarily and do not tire like skeletal muscles.

Muscle growth continues until full development is reached. Exercise also contributes to muscle growth. The fastest-working muscles open and close the eyelids. The busiest muscle is the heart.

Digestive System

The **digestive system** breaks down food to give our body cells energy. Digestion begins in the mouth when the teeth break down food and mix it with saliva. Swallowed food moves down the esophagus, through a tight opening, and into the stomach. Here, food mixes with acid and is digested further to form a semi-liquid called **chyme**. When ready, the chyme is squirted, bit by bit, through the **pylorus**—a valve at the bottom of the stomach—to the small intestine.

The small intestine is about 20 feet (6 m) long and does most of the digestion. Here, chyme mixes with **bile**, as well as pancreatic and intestinal juices. The small intestine filters out useful substances and passes them on to the blood cells. This blood travels to the **liver**, where useful substances are removed and then recombined to meet the needs of the body's cells. The liver also transforms nutrients into glucose, produces the clotting substance in blood, aids in red blood cell production, and filters poisonous materials from blood. Unused substances in the small intestine move to the large intestine, where water and minerals are absorbed. Any remaining waste product, called **feces**, leaves the body through the anus.

The stomach churns constantly. Hunger pangs occur when gas and acid squeeze against the wall of an empty stomach.

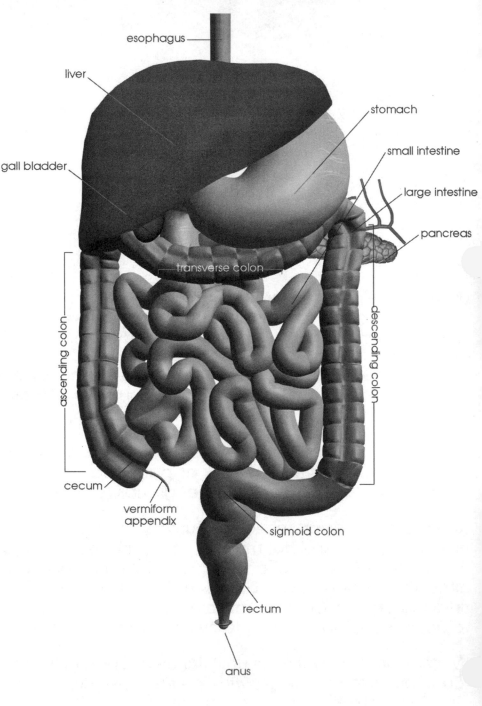

esophagus

liver

gall bladder

stomach

small intestine

large intestine

pancreas

transverse colon

ascending colon

descending colon

cecum

vermiform appendix

sigmoid colon

rectum

anus

Heart

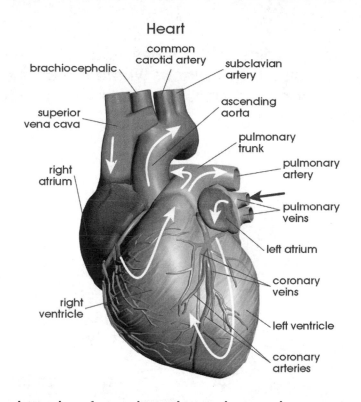

- brachiocephalic
- common carotid artery
- subclavian artery
- ascending aorta
- superior vena cava
- pulmonary trunk
- pulmonary artery
- right atrium
- pulmonary veins
- left atrium
- coronary veins
- right ventricle
- left ventricle
- coronary arteries

The **circulatory system**, which includes the heart, blood vessels, and blood, controls body temperature, helps fight disease, and carries oxygen, food, hormones, and waste throughout the body.

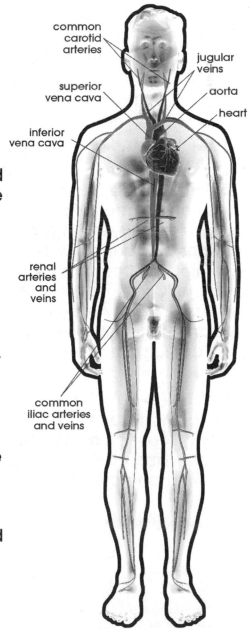

- common carotid arteries
- jugular veins
- superior vena cava
- aorta
- heart
- inferior vena cava
- renal arteries and veins
- common iliac arteries and veins

The heart, a four-chambered muscle, pumps blood throughout the body. Blood high in carbon dioxide enters the heart's **right atrium** from the body's largest veins, the superior and Inferior vena cavas. The atrium pushes blood into the **right ventricle**. The right ventricle pushes blood out the pulmonary arteries to the lungs. Here, carbon dioxide is exchanged for oxygen. This oxygen-rich blood flows through the pulmonary veins to the **left atrium**, then into the **left ventricle**. The left ventricle contracts, pushing blood out the aorta to the arteries. At their smallest points, arteries become capillaries. Here, blood cells deliver oxygen and nutrients and pick up carbon dioxide and wastes. Blood then flows through the veins and back to the heart.

Blood is mainly composed of a liquid called **plasma** that contains water, minerals, proteins, and three kinds of blood cells. Red blood cells transport oxygen and carbon dioxide. White blood cells carry disease-fighting substances. Platelets contain blood-clotting material.

The Heart

Pulse

Each time your heart pumps the blood through veins and arteries, you can feel it! It is called a **pulse**. You can feel your pulse in two places where the arteries are close to the surface of your skin. Gently, place two fingers on the inside of your wrist or on your neck next to your windpipe.

Heart

Place your hand on the left side of your chest. *Lub-dub, lub-dub.* Did you feel it? This is your heart pumping oxygen-rich blood to all parts of your body.

Your heart is really two pumps. It is divided down the middle. Each half of the heart is divided into two chambers. The **right half** pumps blood filled with a waste called carbon dioxide gas into the lungs. The **left half** of the heart takes oxygen-rich blood from the lungs. It sends the oxygen-rich blood to the cells in your body.

What about lub-dub? These are the sounds made by the little "trap doors" called **valves**. The valves open and close to let the blood flow in and out of the heart.

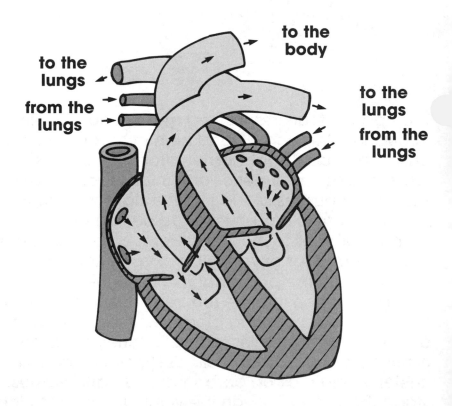

The arrows show the direction of blood flowing through the heart.

Respiratory System

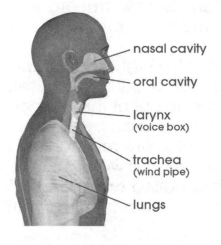

nasal cavity

oral cavity

larynx
(voice box)

trachea
(wind pipe)

lungs

nasal cavity

oral cavity

larynx
(voice box)

primary bronchus

secondary bronchus

trachea
(windpipe)

right lung
(3 lobes)

left lung
(2 lobes)

Through breathing, the **respiratory system** supplies the body with oxygen—a gas needed to obtain energy from food—and rids the body of carbon dioxide—a harmful waste product. Though you may choose to hold your breath temporarily, breathing is an involuntarily process controlled by the brain.

The **diaphragm**, a muscle below the ribs, contracts and moves the ribs outward, causing the lungs to take in air. When the diaphragm relaxes, the ribs relax and the lungs deflate. Air entering the nose is warmed and moistened by mucus-lined sinuses. As it moves to the trachea, the air is cleaned of dirt and germs by mucus and bristly hairs, called **cilia**, lining the nasal passage and trachea. Food and saliva are kept out of the trachea by a flap called the **epiglottis**. From the trachea, air moves down the bronchi and through the bronchioles to the lungs, dead-ending at thin-walled air sacs called **alveoli**.

Alveoli are spongy and surrounded by capillaries. Here, red blood cells give off carbon dioxide and take in oxygen, which they carry to cells throughout the body. The cells use oxygen to create energy and give off carbon dioxide as waste. The red blood cells carry this waste back to the lungs and begin the process again.

The respiratory system, the larynx, and hollow areas in the nose and mouth work together to create sound.

Urinary System

The **urinary system** is the body's main **excretory system**. The central organs are the two **kidneys**, which work to filter waste out of the blood and produce urine.

Blood enters a kidney through the renal artery and flows through smaller arteries into the medulla. Each blood vessel leads to a glomerulus, a tiny looping, twisting tube with small holes in it. Water and other substances leak out of the glomeruli and are collected in nephrons, or filtering tubes. Substances used by the body, including amino acids, glucose, and almost all of the water, are reabsorbed by blood cells. Waste substances, including urea, uric acid, excess water, and salts like ammonia and sodium, are gathered by small tubes called **collecting tubules**. From the tubules, urine passes into the kidney's pelvis, through a ureter, and into the urinary bladder. Urine exits the body through the urethra when the bladder is full. Each day, the kidneys filter about 50 gallons (190 liters) of blood to produce about 1-2 quarts (0.9-1.9 liters) of urine. Your kidneys create less urine when you perspire and more when you drink lots of liquids.

Besides urine production, your kidneys control red blood cell production, make vitamin D for bone development, and help maintain blood pressure.

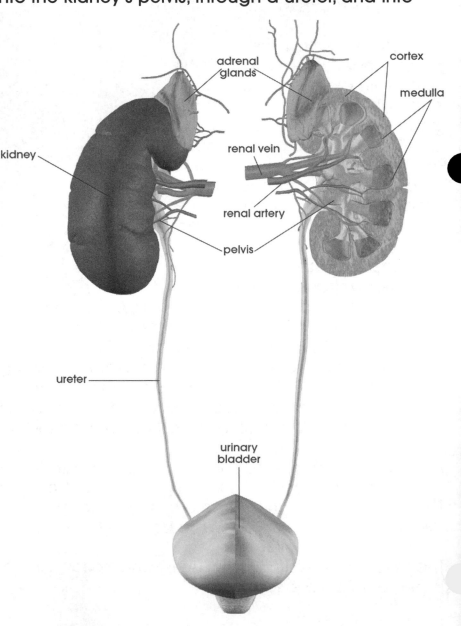

adrenal glands

cortex

medulla

kidney

renal vein

renal artery

pelvis

ureter

urinary bladder

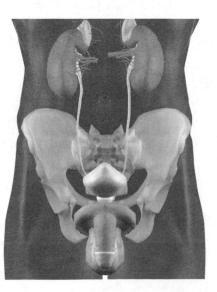

The **nervous system** sends information about touch, pain, temperature, pressure, vibration, and sense of position through the brain, spinal cord, and nerves.

The brain weighs about 3 lbs. (1.4 kg) and requires lots of oxygen to function properly. Each of the brain's three major parts has different responsibilities. The **cerebrum** enables you to think, speak, sense, remember, learn, imagine, and feel emotion. The **cerebellum** assists with balance, posture, and muscle coordination. The **brain stem** subconsciously regulates a number of body functions, such as breathing, blood pressure, digestion, and heartbeat. It also maintains body temperature and warns of hunger, thirst, and fatigue. During sleep, the conscious brain shuts down but the subconscious brain keeps working. The cerebrum and cerebellum are divided into two hemispheres, or halves. Each half of the cerebrum has four small divisions called **lobes**.

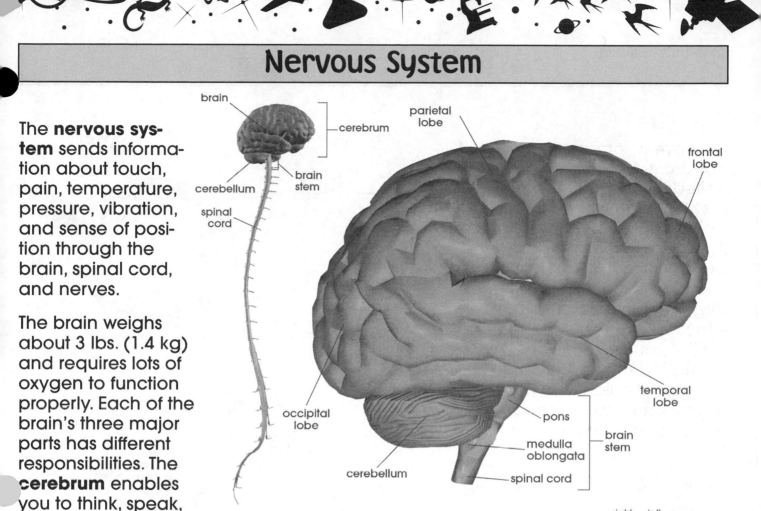

The spinal cord begins at the base of the brain stem and extends down the back. The brain and spinal cord connect to organs through a network of nerves, or bundled neurons. Information gathered by touch and the other senses is sent to the brain or spinal cord along sensory neurons. The information is quickly studied. Then, a message telling the body how to react is carried along motor neurons to the muscles. Most response decisions come from the brain, but reflexes are controlled by the spinal cord. For example, your hand pulls away from a hot object because your spinal cord, not your brain, tells it to.

The Eye

Your eye is shaped like a ball. It has a clear, round window in front called the **cornea**. The colored **iris** controls the amount of light that enters the eye. Light enters through an opening called the **pupil**. In bright light, your pupil is a small dot. In dim light, it is much larger. Behind the pupil is the **lens**. It focuses the light onto the back wall of your eye. This back wall is called the **retina**. The retina changes the light into nerve messages. These messages are sent to the brain along the **optic nerve**. Close your eyes. Gently touch them. They are firm because they are filled with a clear jelly called **vitreous humor**.

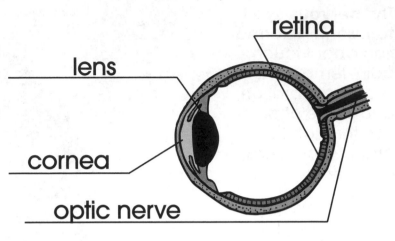

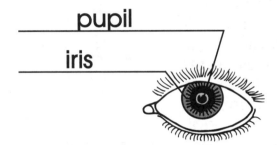

Optic Nerve

One of the most sensitive nerves in your body is the optic nerve. It connects your eyes to your brain. The optic nerve receives messages from other nerves that surround your eyes in the retina. As light is caught in the pupils of your eyes, it is sent to the retina, then to the optic nerve, and at last to the brain.

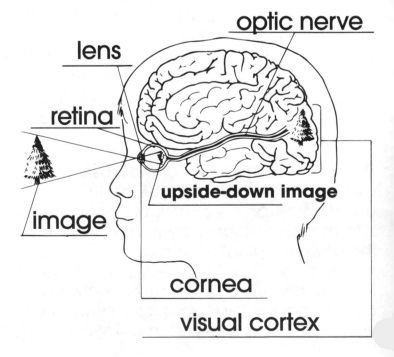

The Ear

A large jet plane rumbles as it takes off down the runway. You can feel the ground vibrate. The plane is also filling the air with vibrations. When the vibrations reach your ear, you hear them as sound.

Your **outer ear** collects the vibrations just like a funnel. The vibrations strike your **eardrum**, making it vibrate, too. These vibrations are passed through a series of three small bones. The last bone vibrates against a snail-shaped tube. This tube is called the **cochlea**. It is filled with liquid. Small hair-like sensors in the cochlea pick up the vibrations and send them to the **auditory nerve**. The auditory nerve sends the sound message to your brain.

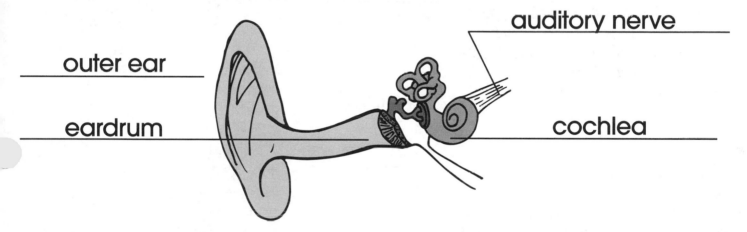

auditory nerve

outer ear

eardrum

cochlea

The Tongue/Taste

Without the sense of taste, many things in life would not be as pleasant. What would it be like if all of your favorite foods had no taste at all?

Your sense of taste is found mainly in the tiny **taste buds** on your tongue. To taste food, it must be chewed and mixed with **saliva**. The taste message is sent to the brain by nerves.

Each of the four tastes has a special center on the tongue. In each center, one of the main tastes is tasted more strongly.

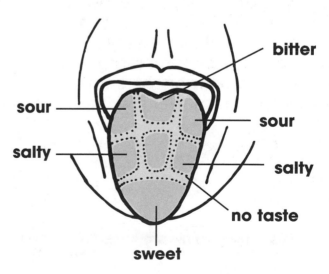

bitter

sour

sour

salty

salty

no taste

sweet

The Nose

The nose is the sensory organ that allows you to smell. When odor molecules enter your nose, they stimulate little hairs called **cilia** to start producing nerve signals. These signals move along the receptors and travel to the **olfactory nerve**, which transmits the signals to the **olfactory bulb**. This is located right below the front of your brain at the top of the nasal cavity. The brain's job is to interpret the nerve signals and identify the smell.

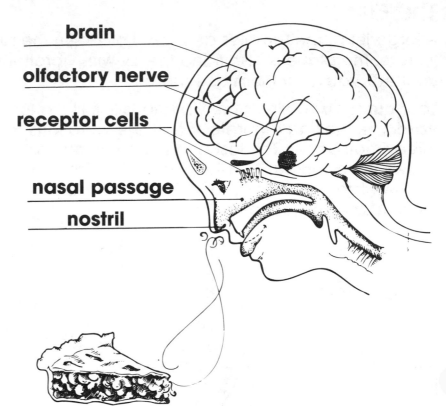

The Tooth

Your first set are baby teeth that come in your first two years. When you are young, your jaw is small. It has just enough room for twenty baby teeth. As you grow older, your jaw becomes larger. The thirty-two permanent teeth push out the baby teeth.

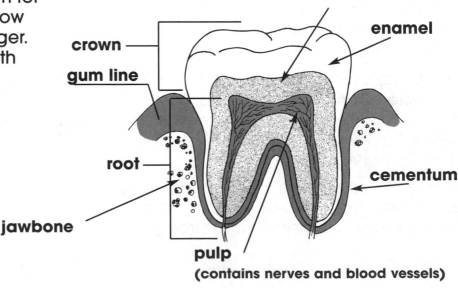

Plant Cells and Animal Cells

Parts of a Plant Cell

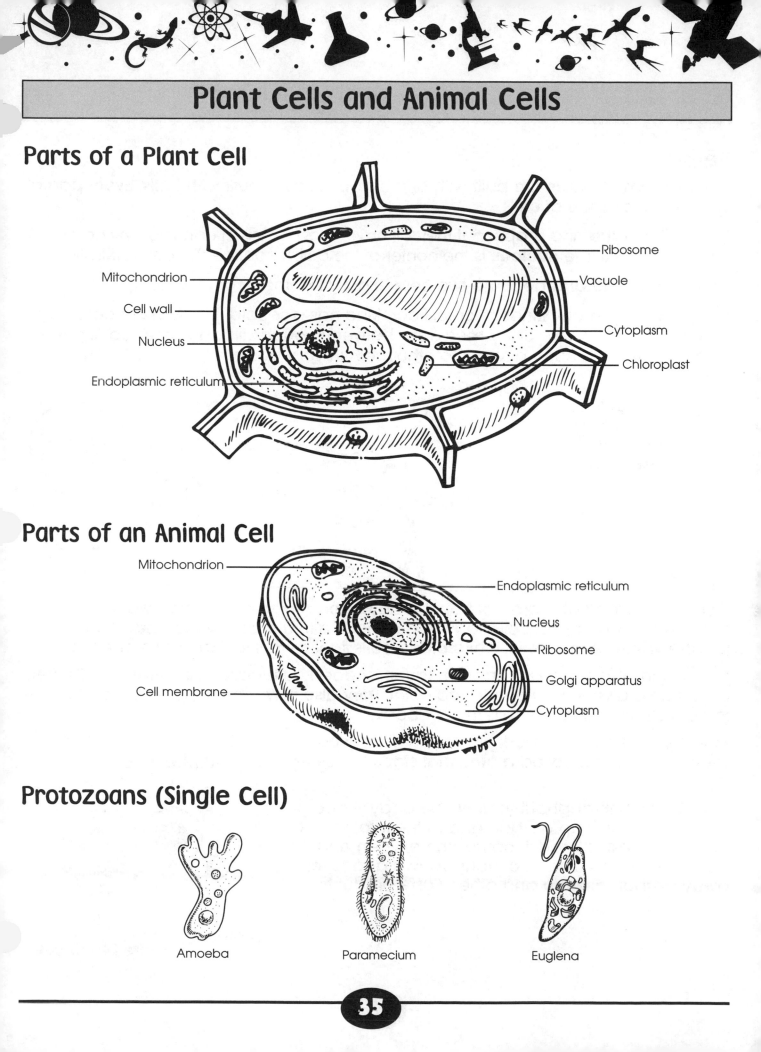

Mitochondrion
Cell wall
Nucleus
Endoplasmic reticulum

Ribosome
Vacuole
Cytoplasm
Chloroplast

Parts of an Animal Cell

Mitochondrion

Cell membrane

Endoplasmic reticulum
Nucleus
Ribosome
Golgi apparatus
Cytoplasm

Protozoans (Single Cell)

Amoeba

Paramecium

Euglena

Types of Cells

Cells

Just like some houses are built with bricks, your body is built with cells. Every part of your body is made of cells.

Cells differ in size and shape, but they all have a few things in common. All cells have a nucleus. The **nucleus** is the center of the cell. It controls the cell's activities.

Cells can divide and become two cells exactly like the original cell.

Your body has many kinds of cells. Each kind has a special job. **Muscle** cells help you move. **Nerve** cells carry messages between your brain and other parts of your body. **Blood** cells carry oxygen to other cells in your body.

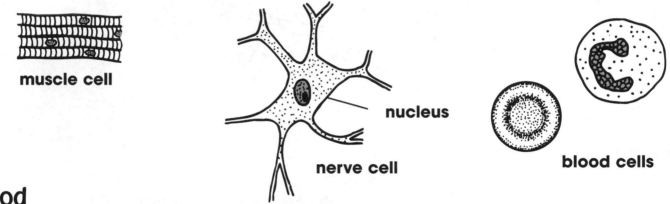

muscle cell

nerve cell

nucleus

blood cells

Blood

If you could look at a drop of your blood under a microscope, you would see some odd-shaped cells floating around in a liquid called **plasma**. These are the **white blood cells**. White blood cells fight germs which cause disease.

You would also see many smaller, saucer-shaped cells called **red blood cells**. Red blood cells give your blood its red color. They also have the important job of carrying oxygen to all of the cells in your body.

Blood **platelets** go to work when you have a cut. They form a plug, called a **clot**, that stops the bleeding.

Blood travels throughout your whole body. It goes to the lungs to pick up oxygen and to the intestines to pick up digested food. It carries the oxygen and food nutrients to all part of your body. It also takes away carbon dioxide and other waste products.

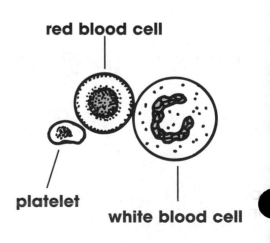

red blood cell

platelet

white blood cell

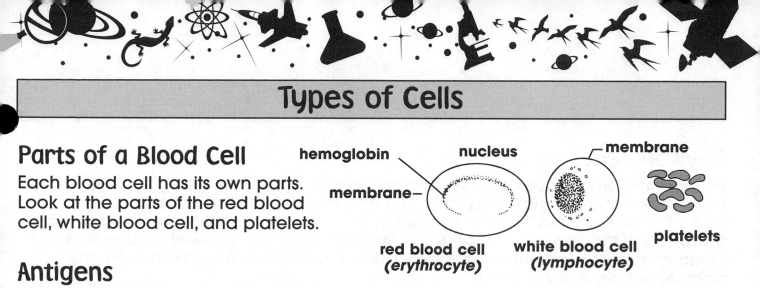

Types of Cells

Parts of a Blood Cell

Each blood cell has its own parts. Look at the parts of the red blood cell, white blood cell, and platelets.

hemoglobin

nucleus

membrane

membrane

red blood cell (erythrocyte)

white blood cell (lymphocyte)

platelets

Antigens

Everyone has a blood type. These types are based on the presence or absence of certain **antigens**, or germ fighters, of the red blood cells. Scientists have labeled these antigens with the letters **A**, **B**, and **O**. Blood types can be combinations of these antigens, like **AB**. Blood types can also be positive or negative, like **A+** or **B-**.

Chromosomes

Your body is made up of cells. Each cell holds threadlike structures called **chromosomes** that contain **genes**. Genes are inherited from your parents and determine how you will look. This is why we often look like our parents. Some genes are stronger, or **dominant**, and some are carried down through generations.

Genes are the parts of cells that determine the characteristics that living things inherit from their parents.

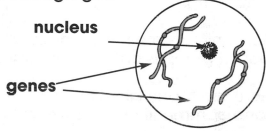

cell

nucleus

genes

Disease

Disease is any uneasiness, distress, or discomfort to any part of the body. Many infectious diseases are caused by an invasion of the body by viruses or bacteria. The word *virus* has Latin origin meaning *poison*. The word *bacterium* has a Greek origin meaning *rod*.

Bacteria are very small, one-celled organisms that may have very serious effects on individuals. Some bacteria are normally found in nature, and some are even found inside the human body. However, if the bacteria not normally associated with a particular part of the human animal invade and begin to flourish, illness results. Viral infection is a particular concern to the human body, for natural defenses are often not in place to combat the viruses, and antibiotics are not effective in fighting them. If natural immunity is not present, the individual simply must rely on the body adapting to the condition by generating new defenses (antibodies) before the virus unbalances the individual's systems too badly. Antibodies may be artificially built up against specific viral infections in the inoculation process. An injection of a small amount of a particular virus causes the body to begin to create antibodies to fight off the foreign invaders. Although the injection of material is small, the body creates a storehouse of the antibodies capable of fighting off subsequent infections by that virus.

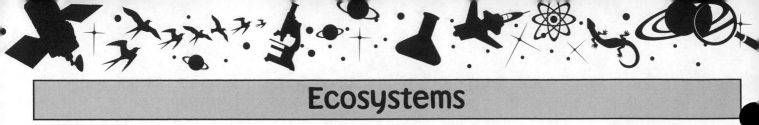

Ecosystems

Environment

An **environment** includes all living and nonliving things with which an organism interacts. These living and nonliving things are **interdependent**, that is, they depend on one another. The living things in an environment (plants, animals) are called **biotic factors**, and the nonliving things (soil, light, temperature) are called **abiotic factors**. **Ecology** is the study of the relationships and interactions of living things with one another and their environment.

Living things inhabit many different environments. A group of organisms living and interacting with each other in their nonliving environment is called an **ecosystem**. The different organisms that live together in an ecosystem are called a **community**. Within a community, each kind of living thing (i.e., frogs) makes up a **population**.

Classifying Organisms

Look at the many living things below. A scientist calls these, and any other living things, **organisms**. Many organisms are alike in some way. They can be put into groups according to the ways they are alike. Putting organisms into groups is called **classifying**.

Most animals are more comfortable living with certain other animals and plants. This special group is called a **community**.

There are many kinds of communities. Some animals live in a forest community or a pond community. Others live in the desert, seashore, or grassland community.

EARTH SCIENCE

Geologic Time

How Old Is Earth?

No one knows for certain how the earth was formed. The most widely accepted theory is called the **protoplanet hypothesis**. According to this theory, a nebula or gas cloud formed about 15 or 16 billion years ago. About five to six billion years ago, the explosion of some huge star or some other huge disturbance caused this gas cloud to spin and collapse. The cloud flattened and turned into a protosun or the beginning of what is now the sun. The particles revolving around the protosun clumped together and formed planetoids. The planetoids had enough gravity to attract smaller clumps of matter and they grew in size. Pressure and temperature increases caused thermonuclear reactions on the protosun and it ignited, turning into a full sun. The planetoids became the planets that revolve around the sun.

Radioactive Dating

Radioactive dating is used to tell the age of fossils and rocks. Another method scientists use is **relative dating**. Scientists do not always need to know the exact age of something. They simply compare two objects to see which is older. This is relative dating. For example, layers of the earth give clues as to the age and composition of life and soil at a given time.

If scientists cut through a layer of rocks and see one layer of rock is sideways or crosscutting, they know the crosscutting layer is more recent because the layers of the earth do not normally go sideways. The crosscutting layer was caused by a volcano eruption, an earthquake, or other geologic disturbance.

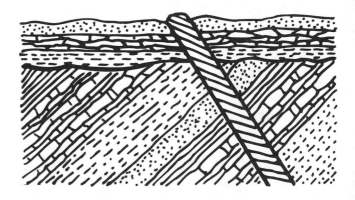

Sometimes the geologic clues do not match up. For instance, sometimes the layers of rock on one side of a river are different from the layers of rock on the other side of the river. This is called an **unconformity**. What might cause an unconformity? What could make a layer of dirt or soft rock disappear?

Geologic Time Scale

The **geologic time scale** is the system scientists have created to divide the earth's natural history into meaningful parts. The geologic time scale starts with the formation of the earth itself and its crust and continues through the beginnings of life on earth up to the present. Scientists disagree about the exact dates of the geologic time scale. One theory is that the earth is 4,568,000,000 years old. The geologic time scale based on this theory divides the time periods into four eras and subdivides those eras into 14 periods, each consisting of millions of years. The geologic time scale is shown below. The Cenozoic Era is the most recent, covering the period from the present to 65 million years ago.

GEOLOGIC TIME SCALE			
ERA	**PERIOD**	**MILLIONS OF YEARS AGO**	**LIFE FORMS**
Cenozoic	Quaternary Tertiary	0–65	Mammals, modern marine animals, herbaceous plants, large carnivores
Mesozoic	Cretaceous Jurassic Triassic	65–245	Reptiles including dinosaurs, more advanced marine animals, and birds (Jurassic)
Paleozoic	Permian Carboniferous (Pennsylvanian+ Mississippian) Devonian Silurian Ordovician Cambrian	245–570	Conifers and modern insects First reptiles Land plants and amphibians Algae, the dominant life form Land plants and fish Primitive invertebrates and algae
Precambrian	Archeozoic Protozoic	570–3,800+	Little evidence of life
	Azoic	up to 4,568 million years ago	Formation of earth and crust

Paleontology

Paleontologists

Paleontologists are scientists who study ancient life and ancient life forms. Fossils buried deep in the earth give clues to the kinds of animals and plants that lived long ago and what their lives were like. Unfortunately, many plants and animals decay long before they become fossilized, so the fossils represent some of the plants and animals that lived on the earth, but not all of them.

Fossils

Fossils are formed in different ways. Sometimes a shell is buried in the mud. A rocky crust forms around the shell. This crust makes a mold. The mold slowly fills with mud or minerals and forms a cast. Sometimes the animal or plant decays but leaves a thin film of carbon behind called a **carbon impression**.

Paleontologists use fossils for relative dating. Some fossils are used as **index fossils**. These fossils were found in many regions for a certain period of time before they became extinct. Trilobites are an index fossil. If the rock layer has trilobites, it may be from the Paleozoic Era. Trilobites first appeared in the beginning of the Cambrian Period and became extinct by the end of the Permian Period.

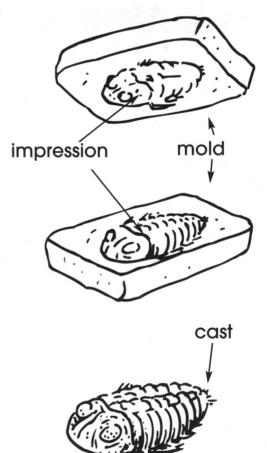

impression   mold

cast

Sometimes paleontologists guess wrong. Fossil remains of a fish called the coelacanth were found in rocks dating up to 400 million years old and some as recent as 60 million years old. No fossils were found after that period, so scientists assumed the coelacanth had become extinct. In 1938, fishermen caught a live coelacanth. In 1987, more of these fish were observed in their natural habitat, which is in the ocean in water over 600 feet deep.

What Are Rocks?

Rocks are **aggregates** or a collection of minerals bound together to make a certain kind of rock. Rocks are classified based on their origin, that is, how they were formed. There are three types or classes of rocks: **igneous**, **sedimentary**, and **metamorphic**. Ninety-five percent of the earth's crust is composed of **igneous** rocks. Igneous rocks come from the magma from volcanic eruptions. Magma is the molten material from inside the earth which is brought up to the surface when a volcano erupts. When magma reaches the surface, it is called **lava**. Many of the igneous rocks form under the earth's surface. Igneous rocks are classified by their texture: glassy, grainy, fine-grained, or smooth. They are also classified by their mineral content. So far, the oldest known rocks found on the surface (not dug up from underground) of the earth are igneous granite rocks from Canada. They are estimated to be 3.96 billion years old. Igneous rocks are either **extrusive** or **intrusive**. Extrusive igneous rocks form when lava from a volcano cools on the surface of the earth. If the lava cools very quickly, it has no grain; rather, it is one texture throughout. Obsidian, a glassy black rock, and pumice, a very lightweight rock, are formed this way. Sometimes the lava cools more slowly, and the rock may have a slight grain as with basalt and rhyolite, two other extrusive igneous rocks. Intrusive igneous rocks are formed when the magma cools underground. Because the rocks cool slowly, small mineral particles form in the rock giving it a grainy or splotchy appearance. Granite is an example of an intrusive igneous rock.

Metamorphic rocks are formed from other kinds of rocks through pressure and heat changes under the earth. In rocks made of one kind of mineral, the mineral grains sometimes move around and the rocks develop a banded or layered appearance as with slate, gneiss, and schist. Sometimes the mineral grains become larger as with marble and quartzite. Sometimes new minerals are formed. Limestone becomes marble, and shale becomes slate. Quartzite comes from quartz sandstone. Metamorphic rocks are classified as **banded**, meaning they have a banded or layered appearance or **massive**, meaning the grains have become larger.

Sedimentary rocks compose about 75 percent of the earth's surface but only about 5 percent of the upper ten miles of the earth's crust. They are formed from hardened layers of sediment that have been weathered or eroded off older rocks. Sedimentary rocks are either **clastic** or **nonclastic**. Clastic rocks are composed of particles of various sizes which have been naturally cemented together. Rocks with large, rounded particles cemented together are called **conglomerates**. Nonclastic sedimentary rocks have been formed from minerals dissolved from other rocks or from organic processes. Coal is formed from decayed vegetation buried for thousands of years.

A Rock Cycle chart in the Appendices further explains rock formation.

What Are Minerals?

Minerals are solid substances found in nature. They are not alive. The atoms which make up a mineral are fitted together to form a crystal. The chemical composition, that is, the kinds of atoms in a given kind of crystal, is the same for every crystal of that kind although impurities or matter that is not part of the crystal may be included. Gold, diamond, rock salt, and the graphite used to make the "lead" in pencils are examples of minerals. Each of these minerals is different, yet many times minerals look like one another or something else. A piece of green colored plastic may look identical to an emerald. A very clear piece of quartz may look like a rough diamond. The Mohs' hardness test, a streak test, color, luster, cleavage, and fracture are all ways of identifying minerals.

Often the **color** of a mineral is the biggest help in narrowing the choices. If the mineral is green, you know it is not sulfur, galena, mica, and many other minerals. Of course, there are many green minerals: emeralds, malachite, beryl, and hiddenite to name a few.

Luster is another way to identify a mineral. Luster is the way the mineral shines. Some minerals have a metallic shine like galena, pyrite, and gold. Other minerals have a pearly shine like opals. Some minerals have a glassy shine like calcite, quartz, and diamond. Some minerals are dull with no real shine at all. Color and luster are not the best way to identify a mineral. Often two totally different minerals can look very similar. **The Mohs Hardness Scale** was developed by a German scientist named Friedric Mohs. It is a list of ten minerals of known hardness. If a mineral is scratched by one of these minerals, you know it is softer than the mineral that made the scratch. If a mineral scratches one of the minerals on the list, you know that the mineral is harder than the known mineral. Diamond is the hardest mineral and will scratch all other minerals.

Another test to help identify a mineral is the **streak test**. For this test you will need a piece of unglazed porcelain. The streak is the color of the mineral in powder form. Some minerals may come in different colors, but if you draw a streak with the mineral on a piece of porcelain, the streak will be the same color for different pieces of the same mineral. Use a guidebook to help you identify the mineral once you have made the streak.

Cleavage and fracture are both descriptions of the way a mineral breaks. Some rocks break evenly with smooth flat planes. This is called **cleavage**. Mica is an example of a mineral with cleavage. It pulls apart into smooth sheets. Some rocks break into irregular or jagged surfaces. This is called **fracture**. Quartz is a mineral that fractures when you split it.

Minerals are classified based on their chemical composition. Silicates, which contain silicon and oxygen, include quartz, hornblende, and feldspar. Carbonates, which contain carbonate (CO_3^{2-}), include calcite and dolomite. Hematite is an oxide and it contains oxygen. Sulfides contain sulfur. Pyrite and galena are sulfides. Sulfates, such as gypsum, contain sulfate (SO_2^{4+}). Halides contain a halogen such as chlorine or fluorine. Halite and fluorite are halides. Native elements are single elements such as gold and silver.

Mohs Hardness Scale

Hardness	Mineral	Common Tests
1	Talc	Fingernail will scratch it.
2	Gypsum	
3	Calcite	Fingernail will not scratch it; a copper penny will.
4	Fluorite	Knife blade or window glass will scratch it.
5	Apatite	
6	Feldspar/Orthoclase	
7	Quartz	Will scratch a steel knife or window glass.
8	Topaz	
9	Corundum	
10	Diamond	Will scratch all common materials.

What Is Geology?

Geology is the study of the earth's composition, structure, processes, and history. It is subdivided into many branches including **mineralogy** or the study of minerals, **paleontology**, **crystallography**, **marine geology** (this is related to oceanography), **planetology** or the study of planets, and **stratigraphy** or the study of sedimentary rock. There are many other branches of geology as well. Some of the knowledge we have gained about the earth has come from indirect observation such as studying the seismic waves from earthquakes and observing magnetic properties of the earth.

Our information on the earth's core has come from indirect observation. The outside of the earth is called the **crust**. The crust is the part of the earth we see, live on, and explore. At its thickest, in the mountains of the continents, it is forty miles thick. At its thinnest, in some places under the ocean, it is three miles thick. We have never penetrated beyond this crust with any machine or person. The deepest mine in Carletonville, South Africa, reaches only 2.3 miles deep into the earth's crust and nowhere near the inner layers of the earth. The mines give us proof that the inner layers of the earth are hot, however. Temperatures at the bottom of deep mines reach 120 degrees Fahrenheit. The crust beneath the ocean is made mainly of basalt. The continental crust is mostly lightweight rocks such as granite. The **Mohorovicic discontinuity** separates the crust from the top part of the mantle. The **lithosphere** is the upper layer of the earth including the crust and the cooler part of the upper mantle.

The **mantle** is about 1,802 miles thick and is composed of silica, iron, magnesium, and other minerals. The **asthenosphere** is hot and plastic or semi-solid and approximately 186 miles thick. It is the layer between the brittle crust and upper mantle and the more solid **mesosphere**. The **core** of the earth consists of the **outer core**, which is about 1,400 miles thick and appears to be liquid. (Remember, we don't know for certain because we can't observe it first hand.) The inner core is approximately 800 miles thick and appears to be solid. It is also very hot, with temperatures between 7,200 and 9,000 degrees Fahrenheit. The whole core seems to be made mostly of iron (which gives earth its magnetic properties) and other heavy elements such as nickel. The **Gutenberg discontinuity** separates the earth's mantle from the outer core.

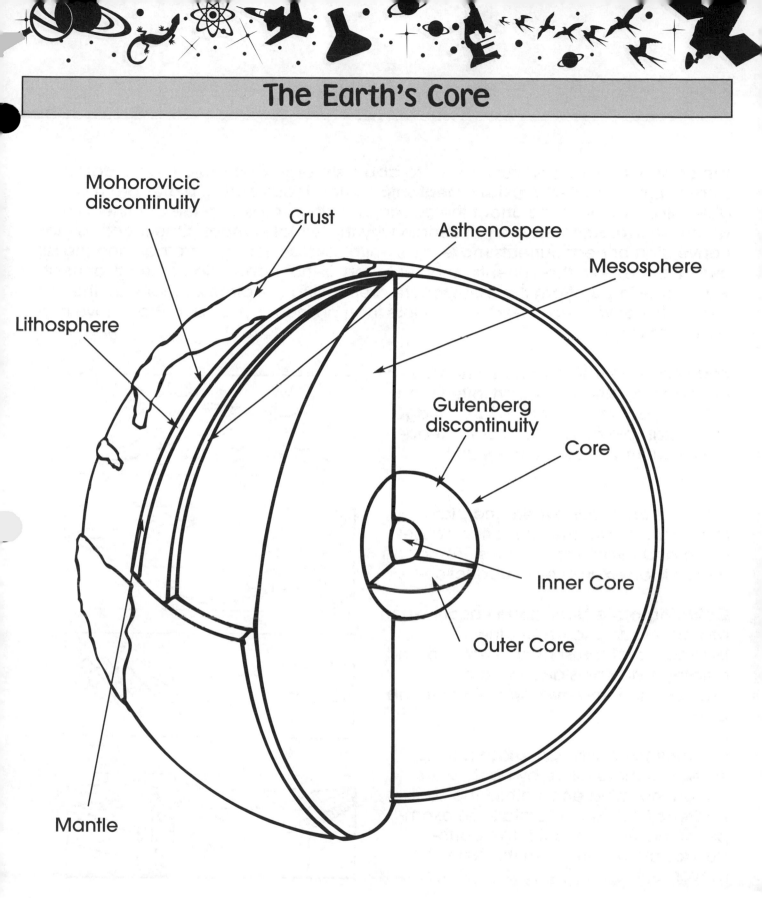

Mohorovicic discontinuity

Crust

Asthenospere

Mesosphere

Lithosphere

Gutenberg discontinuity

Core

Inner Core

Outer Core

Mantle

Tectonic Plates

The crust of the earth is broken up into about six large and more than a dozen smaller pieces called **crustal** or **tectonic plates**. These crustal plates are moveable. Many of them are under the ocean, but others make up the continents on which we live. Scientists are not certain why these plates move. One theory is that convection or heat currents move the semi-plastic asthenosphere carrying the stiff crustal plates with the currents. Another theory is that convection currents or heat waves moving up from the mesosphere are moving the plates. Either way, the plates shift at varying speeds mostly less than an inch a year, and they move in a variety of ways.

Sea-floor spreading occurs when the sea floor literally splits apart, often from volcanic activity. The Mid-Atlantic Ridge is an example of this. Sea-floor spreading frequently causes large earthquakes.

Subduction occurs when one plate moves under another. This often causes deep and large earthquakes. The Japan Trench is an example of subduction.

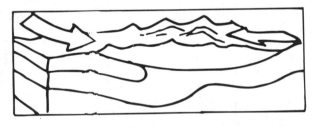

Colliding plate boundaries occur when two plates run into each other. This makes the crust buckle upward and creates mountains and large earthquakes. The Himalayas were formed this way.

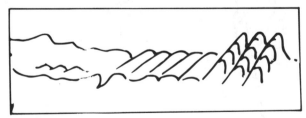

A **transform boundary plate** occurs when two plates slide by each other without harming each other. The San Andreas Fault in California is an example of this. Shallow but large earthquakes often result from this type of movement.

Supercontinent Pangaea

Crustal plates have been in motion for at least 600 million years, possibly for billions of years. The plates move at different rates, but they are constantly shifting. Scientists believe that at one time, a supercontinent called **Pangaea** existed. (Alfred Wegener, a German geologist and meteorologist, suggested this in 1912 when he developed the theory of continental drift. His ideas were not accepted until the 1960s.) Scientists believe the supercontinent broke up into two continents about 180 million years ago. One continent scientists called **Gondwanaland**. It consisted of South America, Africa, Australia, Antarctica, and India. The other consisted of North America and Eurasia and was called **Laurasia**. About 65 million years ago, just about the time the dinosaurs were dying out, the continents began to separate into the continents we have today. Scientists predict that in the next 50 million years, the west coast of North America will separate from the rest of the continent, Australia will move north and join with Indonesia, and Africa and Asia will split apart.

About 250 million years ago the supercontinent called Pangaea looked something like this.

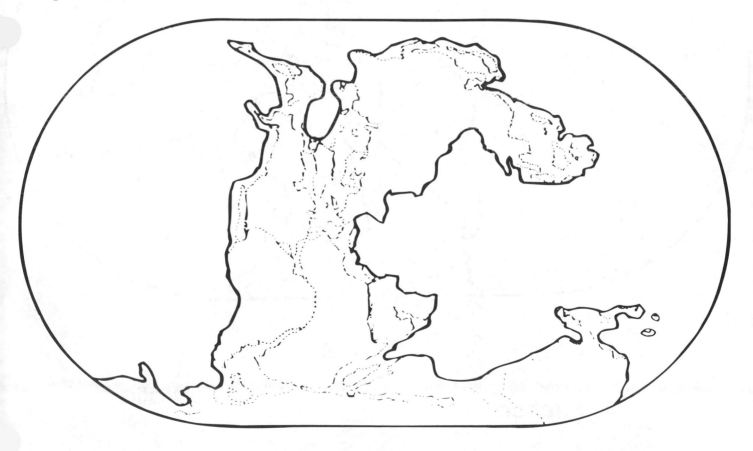

The Continents

By 45 million years ago the land mass split into seven land masses.

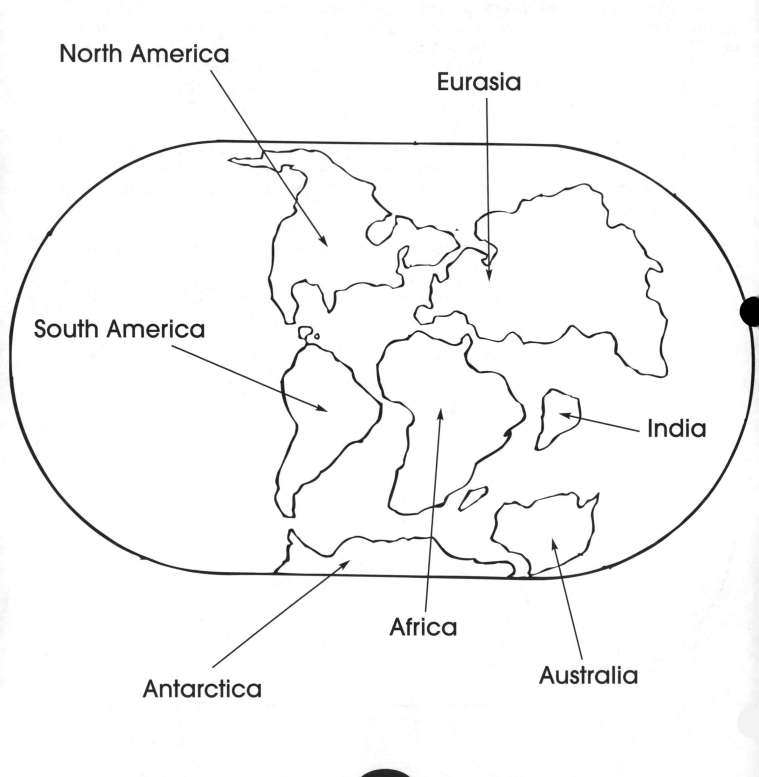

North America

Eurasia

South America

India

Africa

Antarctica

Australia

Landforms

Landforms

Landforms are the features or characteristics of a given landscape. Landforms are classified as one of three things: **mountain**, **plain**, or **plateau**. These basic landforms can have features of their own, including canyons, beaches, and valleys.

A **mountain** is any area of land that rises above the surrounding area. Mountains have been formed by volcanic eruptions, earthquakes, and other strong forces.

A **plain** is a large, flat area. It is a largely grassy area with slow-moving streams. Coastal plains are found near the shore, and inland plains are found in the land-locked interior of the continent.

A **plateau** is a raised, relatively level area that is higher than the land on at least one side of it. If a river runs through a plateau, it tends to make a deep canyon. The Grand Canyon in Colorado is a canyon through a plateau.

The Mississippi River has made a valley in the middle of the Great Plains. Each year tons of loose sediment and topsoil are washed downstream toward the Gulf of Mexico. At the mouth of the Mississippi River, the sediment is deposited, forming a large triangular mound called a **delta**. Part of Louisiana is built from part of this delta.

A chart depicting Landforms is located in the Appendices.

plain

mountain

plateau

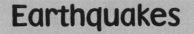

Earthquakes

Earthquakes often occur in the areas where two tectonic or crustal plates come into contact. The place where two plates come into contact or where a plate is splitting apart is called a **fault** or **fault line**. Earthquakes also occur in regions of severe volcanic activity. In this case, the pressure and heat of the exploding volcano causes earthquake tremors or movement.

The **focus** is the point under the earth where the earthquake starts. The **epicenter** is the point on the surface of the earth directly above the focus. The force of the earthquake radiates from the focus in two types of waves. **Body waves** travel outward from the focus in all directions, but they go only through the interior of the earth. **Surface waves** travel outward from the epicenter of the earthquake along the surface of the earth.

Scientists use an instrument called a **seismograph** to record the waves from earthquakes. A stationary pen records the earthquake's vibrations on a sheet of paper attached to a moveable drum. The record of the vibrations is called a **seismogram.**

The measure of how much energy an earthquake has is called the **magnitude**. Magnitude is measured in the United States by a scale called the **Richter scale**. The magnitude is determined by measuring the amplitude or half the distance from the crest to the trough of the largest wave recorded on the seismogram. The scale runs from 1 to 8.8 or 9, but the scale is logarithmic, which means each number represents an increase of ten times over the previous number.

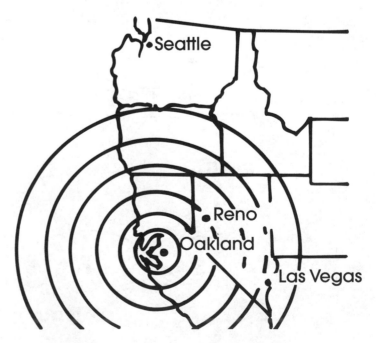

Volcanoes

Magma

Deep within the earth, molten rock, called **magma**, mixes with gases, making it lighter than the surrounding solid rock. The magma begins to rise toward Earth's surface and erupts through a weak area in the crust. The eruption can occur as a violent explosion, propelling lava hundreds of feet into the air. Or, it can gently ooze out the top and side vents of the volcano. There are two kinds of magma, **rhyolite** and **basalt**. Rhyolitic magma is thick and slow-moving. It often traps gases and produces explosive eruptions. Basaltic magma is fluid and faster-flowing. Gases easily escape from it as it gently flows from the vent.

dust

ash

blocks and bombs

crater

vent

conduit

steam and gases

layers of volcanic material from previous eruptions

side vents

lava

crust

mantle

magma chamber

Kinds of Volcanoes

Cinder Cone

Cinder cone volcanoes are formed from cinder and ash that are deposited around the vent after violent explosions. The layers of ash and cinder gradually build a cone-shaped mountain. The Paricutín Volcano in Mexico is a cinder cone volcano that grew to a height of over 1,300 feet in a cornfield.

Shield

Shield volcanoes are formed when lava flows gently from the vent, spreads and builds on a broad, gently sloping mountain. The Hawaiian Islands form a chain of shield volcanoes and include the famous Kilauea and Mauna Loa.

Composite

Composite volcanoes are some of the most spectacular mountains on Earth. These steep-sided, cone-shaped mountains can rise over 10,000 feet. They are made from alternating layers of gently flowing lava, ash, cinder, blocks and bombs. Some of the most beautiful mountains in the world, such as Mount Fuji in Japan and Vesuvius in Italy, are composite volcanoes.

Tsunami

A tsunami is a seismic sea wave. The word **tsunami** comes from the Japanese words **tsu** meaning "harbor" and **nami** meaning "wave." A tsunami is often called a tidal wave, but it is not caused by tides. It can be a much larger wave if it occurs during a high tide, however. Almost 80 percent of tsunamis occur in the Pacific Ocean, approximately 10 percent occur in the Atlantic Ocean, and 10 percent occur in other oceans. Tsunami waves out at sea are only one to two feet high. They can have wavelengths of up to 600 miles, measuring from the crest of one wave to the crest of the next wave. The danger develops when this long wave approaches the shore. The shallow depth of the water causes the wavelength to shorten, and the wave gets taller to compensate for the shorter wavelength. By the time the wave reaches the shore, it can be up to 200 feet high and can be traveling up to 150 miles per hour!

Soil

Soil is a mixture of rock particles and decayed and decaying vegetable and animal matter. The decayed and decaying vegetable and animal matter or organic matter is also called **humus**. Soil containing large amounts of humus is black or dark brown in color. This kind of soil holds water and can be swampy. **Clay** is a smooth-textured soil which tends to be sticky, especially when it is wet. This soil holds water but becomes hard like a brick when it dries out. **Sandy** soil is composed of small rock grains and is very loose and crumbly. It does not hold water well. **Loam** is a combination of humus, clay, and sand. It holds water well. This is good, rich soil for growing many plants.

Soil forms over thousands of years. The type of soil that develops depends on what kind of rock is under the soil, what kind of plants or animals live in and on the soil, the climate, how much the land slopes, and how much time the soil has been forming. Soil forms in layers. A soil that has developed over many years has three layers or **horizons**. The top horizon is a mixture of humus and sediment. It is the layer where plants take root. The second layer is made up of finer particles that have been washed down from the top layer. **Leached** is the term for the particles that have been washed down. This soil has some plant roots. The bottom layer is composed of particles that have been leached from the upper layers and fragments of bedrock. The bedrock lies just under this layer. A **soil profile** is a description of these layers.

Erosion

Often rock and soil particles are moved by water, wind, ice, or even gravity. The process of moving these particles causes holes, gaps, and gullies in the surface of the soil called **erosion**. Water causes much of the erosion. Water flowing over barren soil cuts deep gullies and washes away large amounts of topsoil. The Mississippi Delta, which has formed a large chunk of the state of Louisiana, is composed of eroded topsoil from the land farther up the river. Floods and heavy rains wash off huge quantities of loose soil.

Wind is another factor in erosion. Wind erodes soil either by deflation or abrasion. When the wind blows the dust away, that is **deflation**. This can be a problem in places where the vegetation has been depleted or destroyed. Sandstorms in the desert and dust storms on open farmland (after a period of drought has destroyed the plants) can move a large amount of soil. As the wind blows sand particles against rocks and other surfaces, the sand particles can break off parts of the larger rock or object. This is **abrasion**.

Gravity is the third factor in erosion. As wind and rain erode places on a hillside, large masses of land and rock slide down to lower areas. Rockfalls occur when pieces of rock fall from a high place to a lower place. Landslides are large amounts of rock and soil falling down a mountainside. During a flood, the soil is very wet and is called a **mudflow**. Sometimes the soil moves very gradually. This is called **creep**.

River System

A river may begin its journey to the sea high up in the mountains as a melting glacier or as a number of small streams and brooks high up in the hills. As the river flows downhill the moving water reshapes the land by carrying away sand, stones, and clay. The river and all the water that flows into it make up the **river system**.

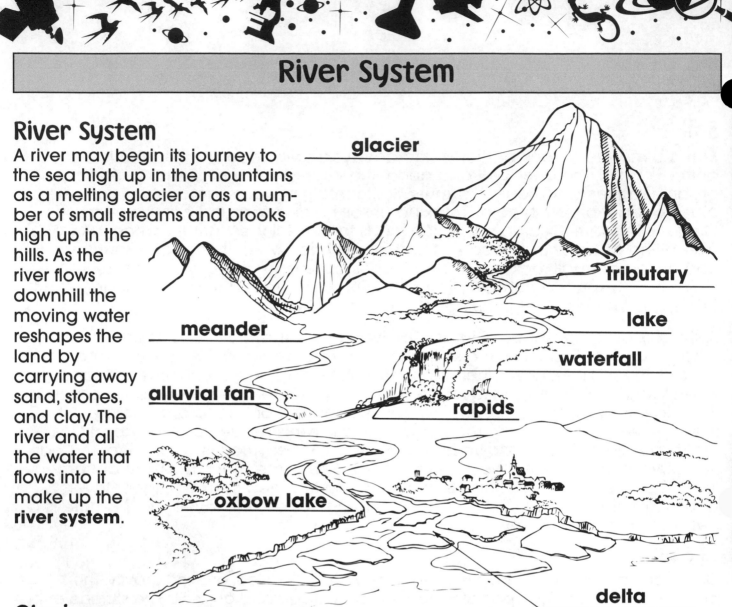

Glaciers

Ice is also a powerful agent of erosion. Many times over recent geologic history, the climate has become cold enough that the snow that fell during a year did not melt before the next year's snowfall began. The accumulation of snow became thick enough that the snow at the bottom of the pile turned to ice and began to flow by being squeezed outward due to its own weight. Over time, enough snow fell that a major portion of the continents were covered, and the climate became very cold. These large ice sheets, sometimes called **continental glaciers**, altered the landscape dramatically in several ways. First, the shear weight of the glaciers themselves crushed the rock beneath them. Today, several of these depressions now filled with water are known as the Great Lakes. The ice also carried a large amount of rock material with it. The land that glaciers moved over sometimes bears the scars of this movement with polished or scratched rock outcroppings, and, in many cases, thin soils. The region where the glaciers stop moving becomes the point at which the glacier deposits much of the rock material and debris it carried. These piles of unsorted sediment, called **till**, are random mixtures of sand to cobblestone to larger sizes of rock.

The Water Cycle

The **hydrosphere** is all of the water that exists on the earth. Seventy-one percent of the earth is water. This includes all of the water in the atmosphere, all of the water underground, and all of the water in oceans, rivers, swamps, lakes, mud puddles, icebergs, and rain puddles. All of this is the hydrosphere. About 97 percent of this water is in the oceans of the earth. A little over two percent is ice. Less than one percent is in the atmosphere, lakes, streams, and groundwater.

The **water cycle** is the process of water moving from one place to another in the hydrosphere. The diagram below shows the water cycle. Water in the ocean or lake evaporates and rises in the atmosphere. The clouds are **condensation** or water vapor collected on small dust or salt particles. The water returns to earth in the form of **precipitation** or rain. Some of the rain sinks into the earth and becomes **groundwater**, and some runs down the hills as **runoff**. The runoff flows through rivers back to the ocean or lake.

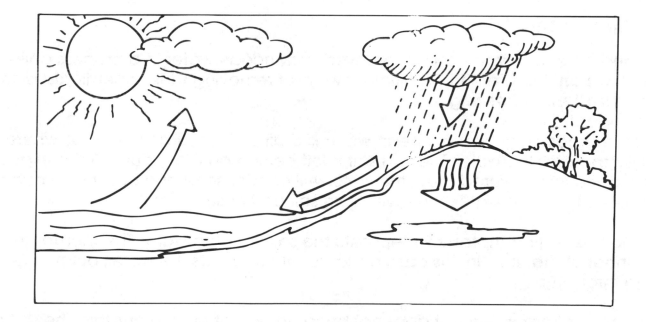

The Ocean

Ocean

An ocean is a large body of salt water. More than 70 percent of the earth's surface is covered with oceans. The Northern Hemisphere has more land surface (39 percent) and less ocean surface (61 percent) than the Southern Hemisphere (81 percent ocean surface, 19 percent land surface). The five major oceans are Atlantic, Pacific, Indian, Arctic, and Antarctic. Gulfs and seas are considered extensions of the oceans and these include the South China Sea, Caribbean Sea, Mediterranean Sea, Bering Sea, Gulf of Mexico, Hudson Bay, Gulf of California, Sea of Japan, Coral Sea, and the Persian Gulf. The Caspian Sea, the Black Sea, and the Red Sea are considered inland seas.

The ocean contains 45 times as much carbon dioxide as the atmosphere. In addition, water evaporated from the oceans comes back to the earth in the form of rain contributing to a major portion of the water cycle. If the oceans dried up, the life forms on earth today would cease to exist. The ocean is approximately 3.5 percent salt. In addition to salt, which is sodium and chlorine, ocean water contains sulfate, magnesium, calcium, potassium, bicarbonate, bromine, and dozens of other chemicals.

Desalination

Salt and other minerals can be removed from ocean water in a process called **desalination**. There are three different ways of removing these chemicals: **distillation, filtration,** or **freezing**.

In some areas of the world, ocean water is drained into large flat areas where the sun evaporates the water. The sea salt is left behind on the ground. If the evaporating is done in a covered area, the water will condense on the cover and can be drained off as pure water. This gives both salt and fresh water.

Filtration uses a membrane to separate the salt from the water. The membrane is a thin sheet of material, in this case a plastic, which allows the water, but not the salt, to go through it.

When water freezes, the salt does not become part of the ice crystals. The salt can be washed off the ice crystals. The ice is then melted into fresh water.

At present, the cost of desalination using any of the above processes makes desalination on a large scale impractical. The amount of energy required to run desalination plants and the cost of transporting the fresh water that is produced are part of the problem. In addition, the plants themselves are expensive to build.

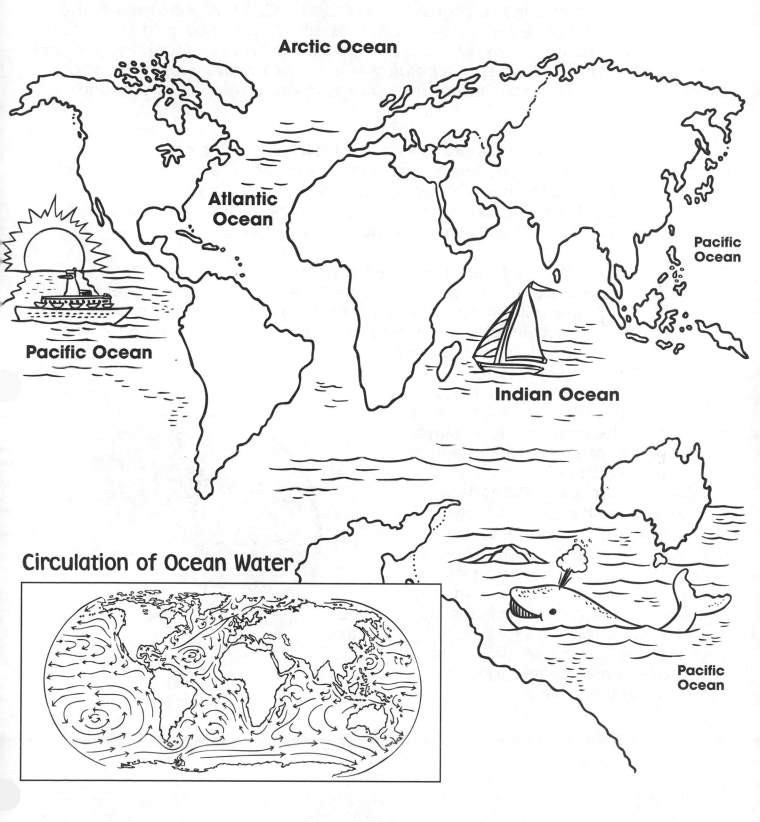

Arctic Ocean

Atlantic
Ocean

Pacific Ocean

Pacific
Ocean

Indian Ocean

Circulation of Ocean Water

Pacific
Ocean

The Atmosphere

A layer of air surrounds the earth. This layer of air is called the **atmosphere**. The atmosphere is composed of a mixture of solids, liquids, and gases. The common gases found in the air are oxygen and nitrogen. The air is 78 percent nitrogen and 21 percent oxygen. The other one percent of the gases includes argon, carbon dioxide, water vapor, neon, helium, methane, krypton, xenon, hydrogen, and ozone.

Nitrogen and carbon dioxide are used by plants to produce oxygen. Then, animals use the oxygen. Ozone forms a layer in the atmosphere that helps protect us from ultraviolet radiation from the sun. None of these gases are weightless. Their combined weight pressing down on the earth is called **atmospheric pressure** or air pressure. Atmospheric pressure is measured with a **barometer**.

The atmosphere is divided into layers. The layer nearest the earth is the **troposphere**. This layer is the air we breathe and the layer where most weather forms. It is approximately five miles thick at the poles and ten miles thick at the equator. The second layer is the **stratosphere**. Because of the layer of ozone, which is in the middle of this layer, the top of this layer is warmer than the bottom. The third layer is the **mesosphere**. The temperature drops dramatically as the height increases in this layer. The fourth layer is the **thermosphere**. Here the temperature rises and the air molecules are spaced very far apart. The top layer is the **exosphere**. It starts at 435 miles above the earth. The **ionosphere** is a layer that overlaps the upper mesosphere and the lower thermosphere. The air in this layer is composed of ions or electrically charged particles which are formed by the sun's radiation. Layers of the ionosphere reflect radio waves and are important to long-distance communication.

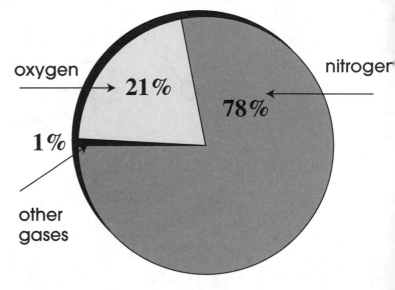

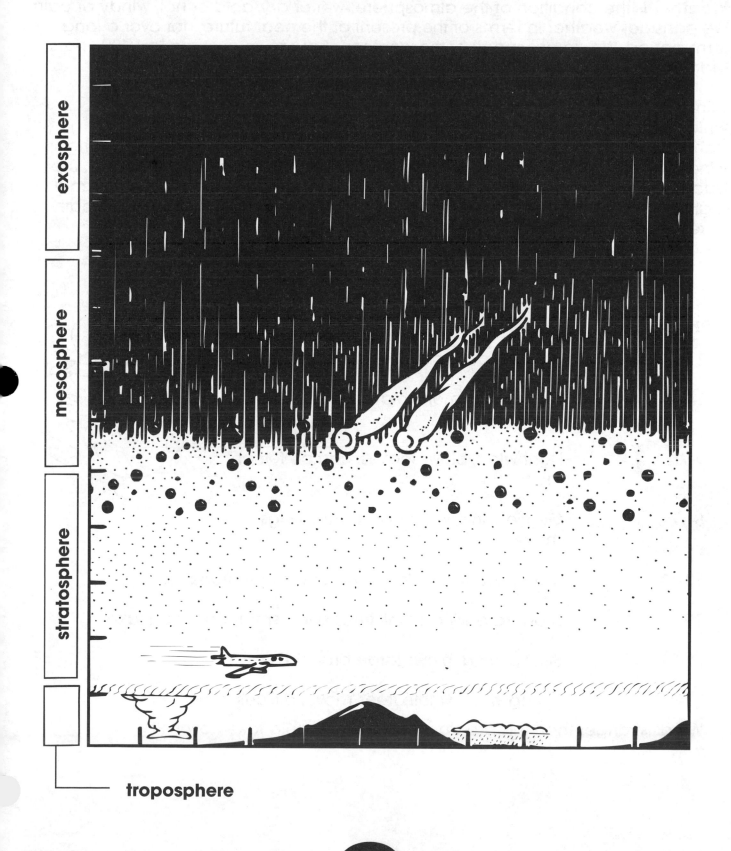

exosphere

mesosphere

stratosphere

troposphere

The Weather

Weather is the condition of the atmosphere: wet or dry, cold or hot, windy or calm. We consider weather in terms of the present or the near future, not over a long-term period. We do not speak of the weather of our town over the last 400 years. Many factors help to cause weather.

Wind or the movement of the air, is measured by the **Beaufort wind scale**, which was devised by Admiral Sir Francis Beaufort in 1806. Since he was an admiral in the navy in the time of sailing ships, he based his scale on how the wind affected the canvas sails of a frigate. His scale was measured in knots. The adapted land scale is measured in miles or kilometers per hour. The land scale is given below. Estimate the wind speed where you are. Listen to the next weather report or check your accuracy with an **anemometer** (an instrument that measures wind speed) if you have access to one.

MPH	Conditions
1	Light wind, smoke rises straight up
1-3	Light wind, smoke blows slightly sideways
4-7	Light wind, blows leaves, can be felt on face
8-12	Gentle wind, leaves and small twigs move
13-18	Moderate wind, blows dust and small branches
19-24	Moderate wind, small trees sway, small waves on lakes
25-31	Strong wind, blows large branches
32-38	Strong wind, whole trees move, difficult to walk

Winds stronger than this are dangerous. You should take cover.

The Weather

Temperature is a factor in determining the weather. Temperatures on the earth vary with the location and the season, but sometimes an area will experience very unseasonable temperatures: warm days in winter and cold days in summer.

Humidity or moisture content of the air is another factor. **Relative humidity** is the amount of moisture in a certain volume of air relative to the maximum amount that volume of air could hold. For example, if the temperature is 90 degrees Fahrenheit and a cubic meter of air is holding 2 grams of water vapor but it could hold 10 grams of water vapor if it were saturated (or holding the maximum amount of water vapor), the relative humidity is 20 percent.

Air masses are large bodies of air with a fairly constant moisture content and temperature. There are two types of air masses: **high pressure systems** and **low pressure systems**. A high pressure system is an area with dense, heavy air. A low pressure system has lighter, less dense air. Air flows from an area of high pressure to an area of low pressure. Between the air masses are the **fronts**. A front is the boundary line between two air masses. It is the front end of the mass of air that is moving into an area. There are four types of fronts: **cold**, **warm**, **stationary**, and **occluded**. Cold and warm fronts are named for the temperature of the air mass that is moving in. Stationary fronts occur when a cold and a warm front meet each other and neither can move. Occluded fronts occur when you have cold, cool, and warm air masses running together.

Air pressure or **barometric pressure** is the force exerted by the weight of the air on everything else on the earth. This force is measured with an instrument called a **barometer**. The air at sea level is on the bottom, so to speak, of the atmosphere surrounding the earth. These molecules are more closely packed, and the air pressure is slightly higher than on mountaintops. The normal pressure at sea level is 29.92 inches of mercury on a barometer or about 14.7 pounds per square inch. Changes in barometric pressure cause wind, and this causes changes in the weather.

Meteorologists, those people who study weather patterns and forecast the weather, use a variety of weather instruments. Some of those instruments are pictured on the next page.

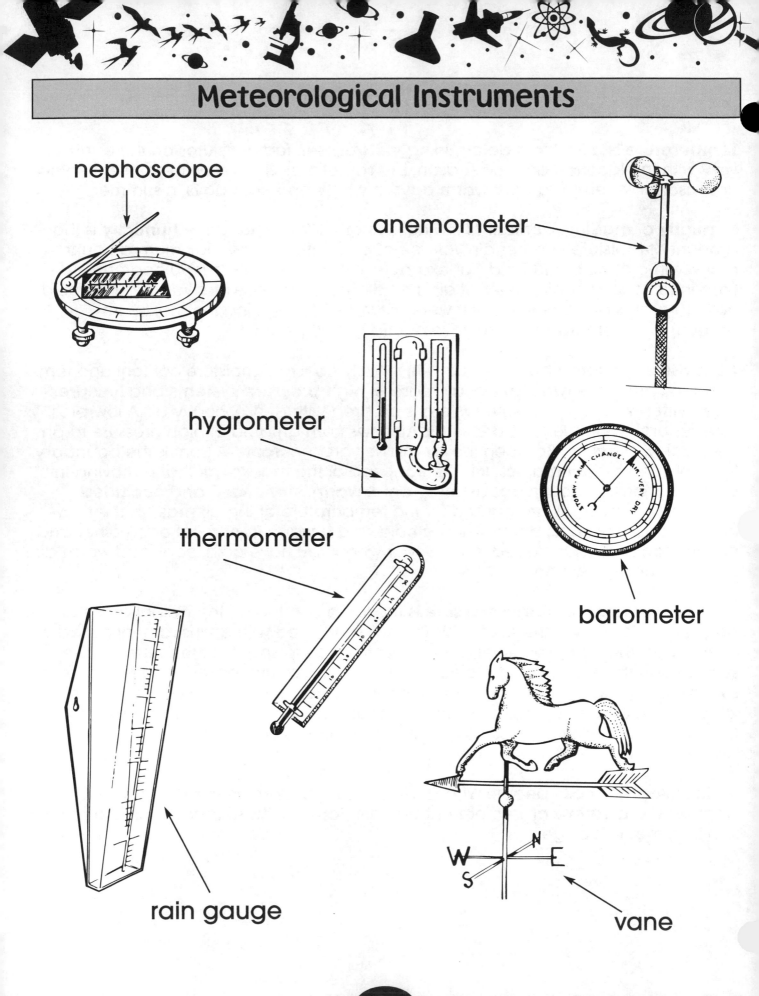

nephoscope

anemometer

hygrometer

thermometer

barometer

rain gauge

vane

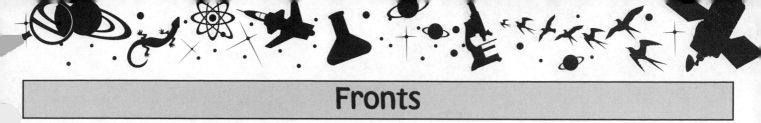

Fronts

Fronts are the borders between air masses. As one air mass moves to be replaced by another, the border passes bringing with it a distinctive weather pattern determined by the nature of the two air masses involved. If the replacement air mass is colder that the first, the boundary, named for the replacement air, is called a **cold front**. If the air mass moving into an area is warmer than what was there previously, then the front is called a **warm front**. If the air masses should become stalled and stop moving, then the front also stops moving. This condition is called a **stationary front**.

Cold fronts, named for the cold air mass replacing a warmer air mass, take on characteristics determined by the way the cold air moves into an area. Cold air is more dense and moves along the surface of the earth throwing the warm air before it high into the air. Its movement is reminiscent of a fast moving bulldozer. The weather associated with this kind of front usually brings "violent" weather conditions, including thunderstorms, as the colder air moves into an area.

Warm fronts signal that warm air, less dense than the air it is replacing, is entering an area. The less dense warm air is not very effective at pushing the denser cold air out of its way. The warmer air tends to slip over the top of the cold air along a very gentle, inclined, frontal boundary. This boundary can extend for hundreds of miles in advance of the warmer air and tends to bring with it a slow moving and gentle period of rain.

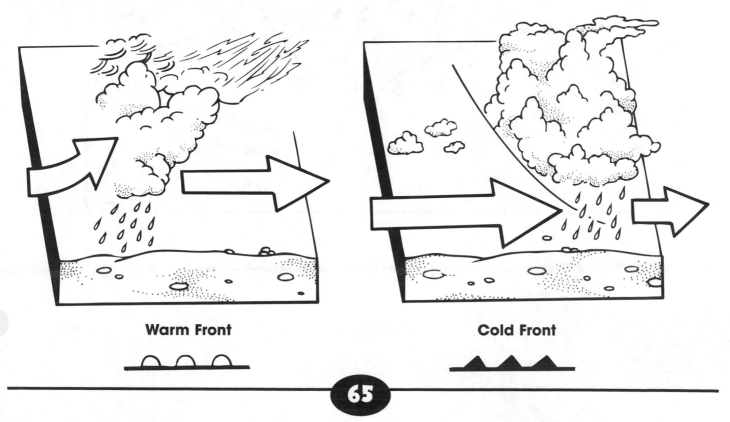

Warm Front   **Cold Front**

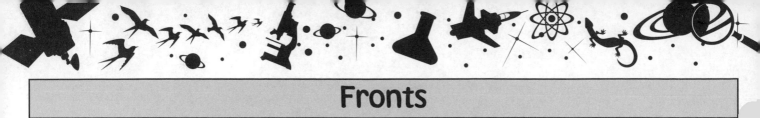

Fronts

A stationary front brings weather that has the characteristics of the front it was originally before stopping, continuing for a longer period of time until it begins to move again. An **occluded front** marks where a cold front actually overtakes a warm front, lifting the entire warm front into the air. It is in this type of front that extreme weather is most often seen, since the entire warm air mass is lifted upward by the more dense cold air mass. The gentle conditions of a warm front are followed by severe weather in this type of front.

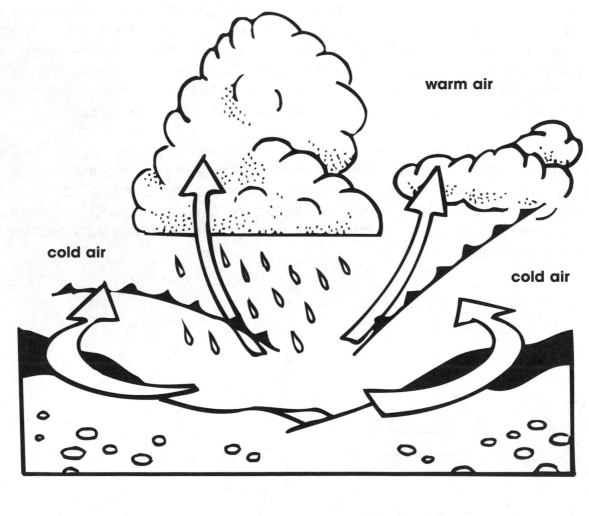

cold air

warm air

cold air

Occluded front

Types of Clouds

Clouds are water droplets which have collected on tiny specks of dust or small salt particles and are suspended in the air. Most clouds form in the troposphere between 1,500 and 40,000 feet from the earth. They form when the water vapor rises, collects on the particles, and condenses or turns to water because of the cooler air temperatures in the upper atmosphere.

Clouds are classified by their shapes. You cannot always predict the weather by looking at the shape of the clouds, but they do give indications of the weather you are likely to see. There are three basic cloud shapes. **Stratus clouds** are layered clouds. These clouds come in layers and often cover the sky. If they are close to the earth, they form a fog. They are thin clouds and usually produce a light drizzle.

Cumulus clouds are thick and puffy. These clouds form on warm days and usually indicate fair weather.

Cirrus clouds are feathery and light. They occur high in the air and are made of ice crystals or very cold water. They are usually fair weather clouds, but they often indicate a change is on the way.

A fourth kind, **noctilucent clouds** are rare clouds. They occur very high in the atmosphere (45 to 54 miles up) and their composition is unknown. They may be meteoric dust or ice crystals. They are usually seen at dusk and may be silver, orange, or blue.

Rainfall

At least 80 inches of rain falls, and thundershowers may occur for 200 or more days each year in a rainforest. **Rainforests** need a lot of rain so that the plants native to them do not dry out.

Dangerous Weather

Rainstorms are not dangerous in themselves unless the ground is saturated or full of water and the amount of rain causes flooding in an area. **Floods** are dangerous to people living in low-lying areas or near streams, rivers, or large bodies of water, which can overflow their banks or change course. Sometimes a cloudburst or very hard rain can cause a flash flood when the ground is not particularly soggy, but the water falls so quickly that the ground cannot absorb it, and most of it runs downhill.

Thunderstorms are localized rainstorms and may be very dangerous due to severe lightning, heavy rain, and large hail. **Hail** may form when a frozen raindrop is blown back up into a cloud. It gets a new coat of water and freezes again. If it is blown back up into the cloud repeatedly, it may become very large. Hailstones as large as a softball have been reported. Hailstones can dent car roofs and even kill animals and people if they are not sheltered.

A **hurricane** or **typhoon** forms over tropical waters; high wind speeds and heavy rain make it dangerous. In a weather satellite, the clouds from a hurricane look like a pinwheel.

A **tornado** is a particularly dangerous swirling cloud which forms a funnel shape. A tornado is the most violent windstorm on earth. A tornado is a whirling, twisting storm that is shaped like a funnel. A tornado usually occurs in the spring on a hot day. It begins with thunderclouds and thunder. A cloud becomes very dark. The bottom of the cloud begins to twist and form a funnel. Rain and lightning begin. The funnel cloud drops from the dark storm clouds. It moves down toward the ground. A tornado is very dangerous. It can destroy almost everything in its path.

A weather chart in the Appendices further explains weather phenomena.

Air Pollutants

People all over the world pollute Earth's air with millions of kilograms of "aerial garbage" each year. The health of plants and animals is greatly affected by these pollutants.

Factories contribute greatly to polluting the air unless environmentally safe practices are followed.

There are also a number of things we can do as consumers to help conserve the earth and the air. Some tips on what we can do to help are listed on the next page.

Conservation

Here are some tips you can follow to help conserve the earth and the air.

1. Buy dry groceries in cardboard boxes made from recycled material.
2. Riding a bike saves energy and reduces pollution.
3. Refuse to buy excessively packaged products and reuse and recycle what you can.
4. Write a letter to a company doing something environmentally harmful and ask its people to change their ways.
5. Help reduce needless waste by not purchasing products with excessive packaging.
6. Mix waste foods with dirt to make a compost pile that will help plants grow.
7. Know what you want from the refrigerator before you open the door so energy will not be wasted by the door being open too long.
8. Look for spray bottles rather than aerosols that are non-recyclable and fill up landfills which contribute to air pollution.
9. Lessen water pollution by eating vegetables that do not have chemicals sprayed on them that can often be washed into streams.
10. Dispose of hazardous waste materials at a site set aside for them.
11. Just because you are outside on a picnic doesn't mean you have to use throwaway plates and cups.
12. Reduce your heating bill and energy usage by sealing off drafts and checking the insulation in your home.
13. Recycle paper by using the back of a sheet of paper.
14. Plant a tree to help hold the ground.
15. Batteries contain hazardous materials which can leak into landfills when thrown away, so use rechargeable ones.
16. Set up a recycling center in your home and recycle newspapers, glass, and aluminum.
17. Take bags to the store when you shop and fill them with what you buy rather than taking more bags home and throwing them away.
18. Turn tap water on and off as you need it when brushing your teeth.
19. Turn off lights when you are not using them to cut down on your electric bill and energy usage.
20. You can tell if a product or package is made from recyclable materials if it is gray or dark brown—not white.

Astronomy

Introduction

Astronomy is the study of the universe. It is the study of planets, satellites, stars, and galaxies and everything related to them. Since we cannot travel to most of these places, much of our knowledge comes from observation and from space probes and man-made satellites sent up to collect data as well as from telescopes, binoculars, and the eyes of observant people. Many of the great discoveries in astronomy have been made by amateurs who took the time to observe the sky closely on a regular basis.

Our Solar System

Our **solar system** is made up of the sun and all the objects that go around, or **orbit**, the Sun.

The Sun is the only star in our solar system. It gives heat and light to the nine planets in the solar system. The planets and their moons all orbit the Sun.

The time it takes for each planet to orbit the Sun is called a **year**. A year on Earth is 365 days. Planets closer to the Sun have shorter years. Their orbit is shorter. Planets farther from the Sun take longer to orbit, so their years are longer. A year on Pluto is 248 of our years!

Asteroids, comets, and meteors are also part of our solar system.

Our Sun

If we could travel from the Sun's **core**, or center, to the surface we would be at the **photosphere**, which is the surface part of the Sun seen from Earth. Flashes of light seen by scientists on the surface of the Sun are called **flares**, and dark patches are called **sunspots**. Sometimes eruptions of gas, called **prominences**, can also be seen during a solar eclipse. Just above the Sun's surface is a layer of bright gases called the **chromosphere**. The **corona**, the region beyond the chromosphere, consists of white concentric circles of light that radiate from the Sun.

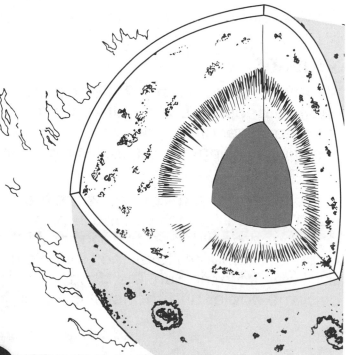

Earth

Earth's Axis

Earth spins about an imaginary line that is drawn from the North Pole to the South Pole through the center of the Earth. This line is called Earth's **axis**. Instead of using the word "spin," though, we say that Earth **rotates** on its axis.

Earth rotates one time every 24 hours. The part of Earth facing the Sun experiences day. The side that is away from the Sun's light experiences night.

Earth's Rotation and Revolution

Earth travels in a path around the Sun called its **orbit**. Earth's orbit is almost 620 million miles. It takes 1 year, or 365 days, for the Earth to orbit or **revolve** around the Sun.

Earth's orbit is not a perfect circle. It is a special shape called an **ellipse**.

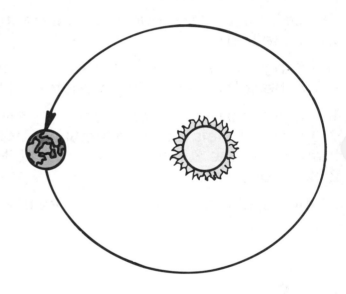

Seasons

Why do seasons change? The seasons change because Earth is tilted like the Leaning Tower of Pisa. As Earth orbits the Sun, it stays tilting in the same direction in space.

In the Northern Hemisphere, when the North Pole is tilting toward the Sun, the days become warmer and longer. It is summer. Six months later, the North Pole tilts away from the Sun. The days become cooler and shorter. It is winter.

Moon

Earth

Earth is a very special planet because it is the only planet known to have life. Only Earth has the necessities to support life—water, air, moderate temperatures, and suitable air pressure. Earth is about 92,960,000 miles from the Sun and is 7,926 miles in diameter. Its highest recorded temperature was 136°F in Libya and the lowest was -127°F in Antarctica.

Moon

As the Moon orbits Earth, we often see different amounts of the Moon's lighted part. Sometimes it looks like a circle, half-circle or thin curved sliver. These different shapes are the Moon's **phases.** There are eight distinct phases. The phases designate both the degree to which the Moon is illuminated and the geometric appearance of the illuminated part. The **New Moon** is the Moon's unilluminated side facing the Earth. The Moon is not visible (except during a solar eclipse). The **Waxing Crescent** is when the Moon appears to be partly but less than one-half illuminated by direct sunlight. The fraction of the Moon's disk that is illuminated is increasing. The **First Quarter Moon** appears to be illuminated by direct sunlight. The fraction of the Moon's disk that is illuminated is increasing. **Waxing Gibbous** is the term used when the Moon appears to be more than one-half but not fully illuminated by direct sunlight. The fraction of the Moon's disk that is illuminated is increasing. The **Full Moon** is when the Moon's illuminated side faces the Earth. The Moon appears to be completely illuminated by direct sunlight. The **Waning Gibbous Moon** appears to be more than one-half but not fully illuminated by direct sunlight. The fraction of the Moon's disk that is illuminated is decreasing. In the **Last Quarter**, one-half of the Moon appears to be illuminated by direct sunlight. The fraction of the Moon's disk that is illuminated is decreasing. The last phase is the **Waning Crescent**. The Moon appears to be partly but less than one-half illuminated by direct sunlight. The fraction of the Moon's disk that is illuminated is decreasing.

Moon Surface

Scientists have studied the rocky surface of the **Moon**, our closest neighbor in space. By studying samples the astronauts have brought back to Earth, we know the Moon is probably $4\frac{1}{2}$ billion years old! They also know the Moon is very different from the earth. Large holes on the surface of the Moon are called **craters**. Scientists have discovered the Moon has no air or gravity and no wind or water. Because of this, everything stays the same on its surface. The U.S. flag placed on the Moon by our astronauts should stay for millions of years. That means future visitors on the Moon will see it long after we are gone.

Lunar and Solar Eclipses

Lunar Eclipse

When the Sun, Earth, and Moon are in direct line, the Moon moves into Earth's shadow causing a **lunar eclipse**.

Solar Eclipse

When the new moon is directly between the Earth and the Sun, an eclipse of the Sun occurs. The type of **solar eclipse** that occurs depends on how much sunlight the Moon blocks from the view on Earth.

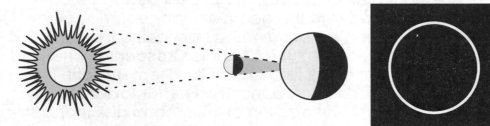

total eclipse

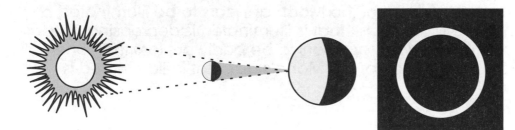

annular eclipse

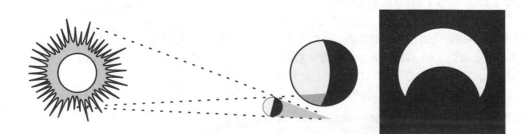

partial eclipse

The Sun

The Sun makes up 99.86 percent of the mass of our solar system. Sixty percent of the Sun is its hot **core**, which is about 248,560 miles in diameter. The core temperatures reach 27,000,000 degrees Fahrenheit. Immediately outside of the core is the **radioactive zone**, followed by the **convective zone**, a layer of gases that moves the heat from the core to the outer layers of the Sun. The **photosphere** is the outer layer of the Sun that is normally visible to us. The photosphere has sunspots or cooler spots that appear darker than the rest of the surface and plages, which are super-hot, bright spots. The Sun also has **solar flares**, which make bursts of fire and prominences, which are loops or fountain-shaped swirls of fire. The **corona** is the halo-like layer of the sun that is visible only during a solar eclipse.

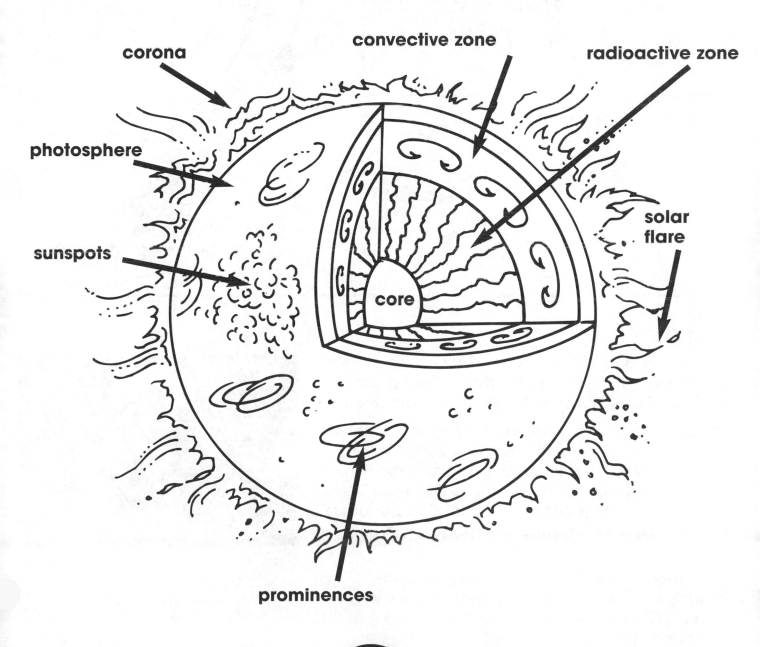

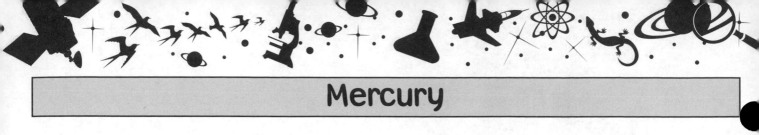

Planet Size

Planets very greatly in size.

Planet	Diameter
Mercury	3,000 miles
Venus	7,500 miles
Earth	7,900 miles
Mars	4,200 miles
Jupiter	88,700 miles
Saturn	74,600 miles
Uranus	31,600 miles
Neptune	30,200 miles
Pluto	1,900 miles

Diameter means distance through the middle.

Mercury

Mercury is one of the smallest of the nine planets in our solar system. It is also the nearest planet to the Sun. It is about 35,9980,000 miles from the Sun.

Mercury spins very slowly. The side next to the Sun gets very hot before it turns away from the Sun. The other side freezes while away from the Sun. As the planet slowly spins, the frozen side then becomes burning hot and the hot side becomes freezing cold. Its temperature ranges from −315°F to 648°F.

Even though Mercury spins slowly, it moves around the Sun very quickly. That is why it was named Mercury—after the Roman messenger for the gods.

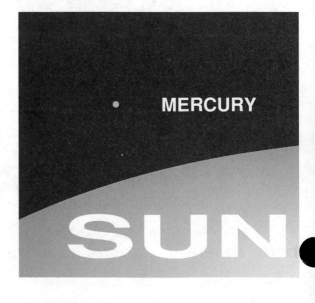

MERCURY

SUN

Venus

Venus is the planet nearest to Earth. It is about 67,230,000 miles from the Sun. Because it is the easiest planet to see in the sky, it has been called the morning star and evening star. The Romans named Venus after their goddess of love and beauty. Venus is sometimes called "Earth's twin." It is the brightest planet in the sky, as seen from Earth, and is brighter even than the stars.

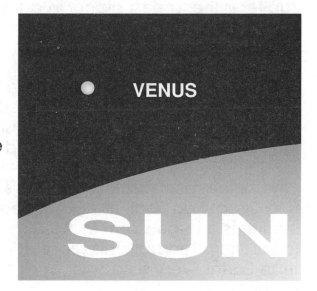

Venus is covered with thick clouds. The Sun's heat is trapped by the clouds. The temperature on Venus is nearly 900°F!

Space probes have been sent to study Venus. They have reported information to scientists. But they can only last a few hours on Venus because of the high temperature.

Venus turns in the opposite direction from Earth. So, on Venus, the Sun rises in the west and sets in the east!

Mars

Mars is the fourth planet from the Sun at 141,600,000 miles. The diameter of Mars is 4,200 miles. Mars is often called the Red Planet because rocks on its surface contain limonite, which is similar to rust. Mars has two moons.

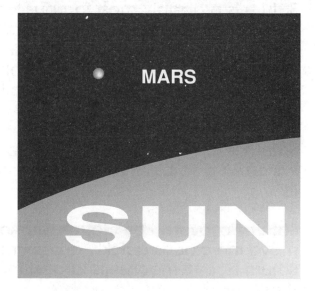

Mars is dustier and drier than any desert on Earth. However, new evidence suggests that Mars may have once been a wetter and warmer planet. According to information gathered at the 1997 landing site of the Mars Pathfinder Mission, there may have been tremendous flooding on Mars about 2 to 3 billion years ago. Mars, then, may once have been more like Earth than was earlier thought.

Jupiter and Saturn

Jupiter

Jupiter is the largest planet in our solar system. It has sixteen moons. Jupiter is the second-brightest planet—only Venus is brighter.

Jupiter is bigger and heavier than all of the other planets together. It is covered with thick clouds. Many loose rocks and dust particles form a single, thin, flat ring around Jupiter.

One of the most fascinating things about Jupiter is its Great Red Spot. The Great Red Spot of Jupiter is a huge storm in the atmosphere. It looks like a red ball. This giant storm is larger than Earth! Every six days it goes completely around Jupiter.

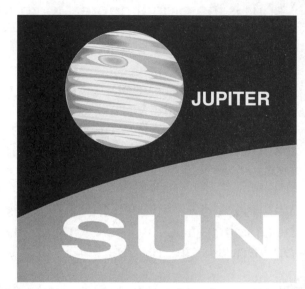

JUPITER

SUN

Saturn

Saturn is probably most famous for its rings. These rings are made of billions of tiny pieces of ice and dust. Although these rings are very wide, they are very thin. If you look at the rings from the side, they are almost too thin to be seen.

Saturn is the second-largest planet in our solar system. It is so big that 758 Earths could fit inside it!

Saturn is covered by clouds. Strong, fast winds move the clouds quickly across the planet. Saturn has 18 moons! Its largest moon is called Titan.

SATURN

SUN

Uranus and Neptune

Uranus

Did you know that Uranus was first thought to be a comet? Many scientists studied the mystery comet. It was soon decided that Uranus was a planet. It was the first planet to be discovered through a telescope.

Scientists believe that Uranus is made of rock and metal with gas and ice surrounding it.

Even through a telescope, Uranus is not easy to see. That is because it is almost two billion miles from the sun that lights it. It takes Uranus 84 Earth years to orbit the Sun!

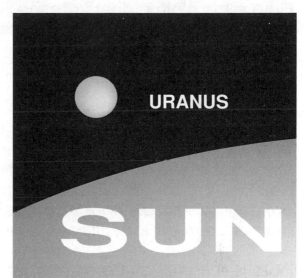

Scientists know that Uranus has fifteen moons and is circled by ten thin rings. But there are still many mysteries about this faraway planet.

Neptune

Neptune is the eighth planet from the Sun. It is difficult to see Neptune—even through a telescope. It is almost three billion miles from Earth.

Scientists believe that Neptune is much like Uranus—made of rock, iron, ice, and gases.

Neptune has eight moons. Scientists believe that it may also have several rings.

Neptune is so far away from the Sun that it takes 164 Earth years for it to orbit the Sun just once! Scientists still know very little about this cold and distant planet.

Pluto

Pluto is the ninth planet from the Sun. It is farther from the Sun than any other planet.

If you stood on Pluto, the Sun would look just like a bright star in the sky. Pluto is so far away that it gets little of the Sun's heat. That is why it is freezing cold on Pluto.

Some scientists think that Pluto was once one of Neptune's moons that escaped from orbit and drifted into space. Other scientists believe it has always been a planet in our solar system.

Pluto is so far away from the sun that it takes 247 Earth years just to orbit the Sun once!

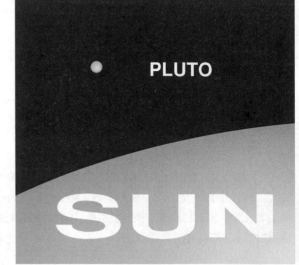

The Asteroids

The asteroids are extremely small bodies that travel mainly between the orbits of Mars and Jupiter. There are thousands of them, and new ones are constantly being discovered.

Many asteroids are made of dark, rocky material, have irregular shapes, and range widely in size. Ceres, the largest and first-known asteroid, is about 600 miles in diameter. Hildago, another asteroid, is only about nine miles in diameter. Because the asteroids' orbits change slowly due to the gravitational attraction of Jupiter and other large planets, asteroids sometimes collide with each other. Fragments from these collisions can cause other collisions. Any resulting small fragments that reach the surface of Earth are called **meteorites**.

Black Holes and Comets

Black Holes

Have you ever heard of a mysterious black hole? Some scientists believe that a black hole is an invisible object somewhere in space. Scientists believe that it has such a strong pull toward it, called **gravity**, that nothing can escape from it!

These scientists believe that a black hole is a star that has collapsed. The collapse made its pull even stronger. It seems invisible because even its own starlight cannot escape! It is believed that anything in space that comes near the black hole will be pulled into it forever. Some scientists believe there are many black holes in our galaxy.

Comets

Planets and moons are not the only objects in our solar system that travel in orbits. Comets also orbit the sun.

A **comet** is like a giant dirty snowball that is $\frac{1}{2}$ to 3 miles wide. It is made of frozen gases, dust, ice, and rocks.

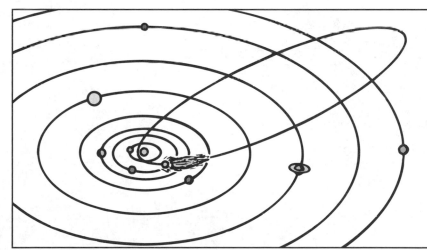

As the comet gets closer to the Sun, the frozen gases melt and evaporate. Dust particles float in the air. The dust forms a cloud called a **coma**. The "wind" from the Sun blows the coma away from the Sun. The blowing coma forms the comet's tail.

There are more than 800 known comets. Halley's Comet is the most famous. It appears about every 76 years. The last scheduled appearance in this century was in 1985.

Galaxy

Milky Way Galaxy

Our Earth and Sun belong to a vast number of stars called the Milky Way Galaxy. The word *galaxy* comes from a Greek word meaning *milk*.

The Milky Way galaxy is made up of the Earth, its solar system, and all the stars you can see at night. There are over 100 billion stars in the Milky Way!

The Milky Way is shaped much like a C.D. It has a center which the outer part goes around. Galaxies have several different shapes.

The Milky Way is always spinning slowly through space. It is so large that it would take 200 million years for the galaxy to make one complete turn.

Many stars in the Milky Way are in clusters. Some star clusters contain up to one million stars!

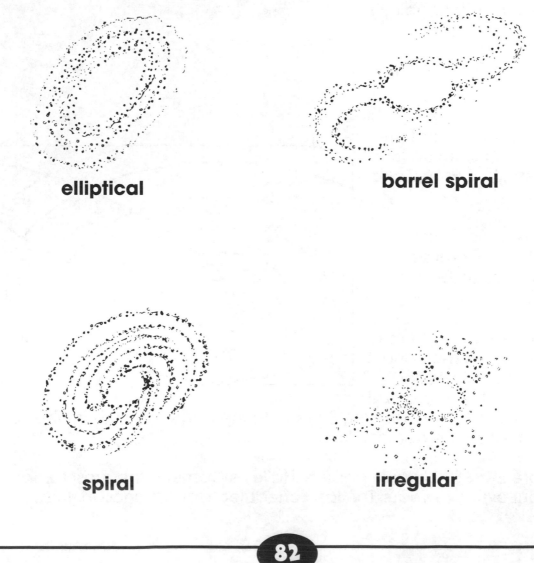

elliptical

barrel spiral

spiral

irregular

Constellations

On a clear night, you can see about two thousand stars in the sky. Scientists can use giant telescopes to see billions of stars.

Constellations are the outline of patterns of objects traced among groups of stars in the night sky. The word *constellation* comes from Latin words meaning *together* and *stars*. Even though the stars in a constellation are thought of as belonging to the same group, the stars actually may be extremely far apart. Astronomers have divided the sky into 88 constellations

Ancient people named many constellations for animals, heroes, and mythical creatures. Many of these names are still used.

Some constellations can be seen every night of the year. Others change with the seasons.

Since all stars are constantly moving, these same constellations that we now see will be changed thousands of years from now.

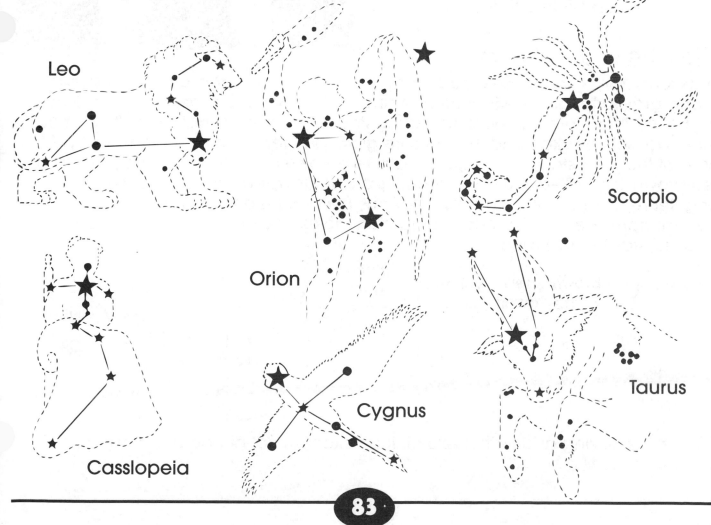

Leo

Orion

Scorpio

Casslopeia

Cygnus

Taurus

Stars

Our Sun

Our Sun is a star. It is not one of the largest or brightest stars. It is a fiery, glowing ball of burning gases. All stars are composed of burning gases. Many of them are much larger than our Sun. Betelgeuse, in the constellation Orion, is so large that if it were in the place of our Sun it would fill the space out past the orbit of Mars. Betelgeuse is about 520 light years away from us. That means the light you see shining from Betelgeuse tonight is actually the light that left Betelgeuse 520 years ago.

Some stars are hotter than others and this makes them glow a different color. The hottest stars may burn up to 50,000 degrees Centigrade or 90,000 degrees Fahrenheit. These super hot stars are a blue-white color. The coolest stars are a brown color and burn a cool 2,100 degrees Centigrade or 3,800 degrees Fahrenheit.

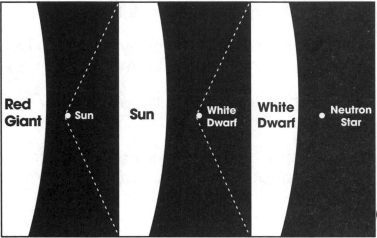

Life of a Brown Dwarf

Stars form from very dense clouds of dust and gas. These dense clouds have a strong gravitational force that attracts any dust particles or gases that come near and bring them into the mass increasing its size. The core of this cloud becomes more densely packed and the pressure grows, the temperatures increase, and the core of the protostar starts to glow a dull red-brown color. If the star stays small and red-brown, it is called a **brown dwarf**. As a star grows hotter, the color becomes a brighter red. When the core gets super hot, nuclear fusion of hydrogen atoms into helium atoms begins. This nuclear reaction makes the star glow a bright red for the smallest star, the **red dwarf**.

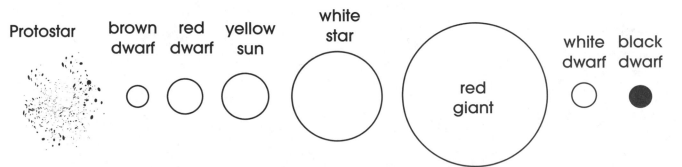

A chart displaying and further explaining astronomical phenomena appears in the Appendices.

PHYSICAL SCIENCE

Physical Science

Physical science includes the natural sciences of physics and chemistry that deal primarily with nonliving materials.

Electricity

Televisions, radios, toasters, lights, and many other household items run on **electric current**. Electric current is the continuous flow of electrons from a source. **Static electricity** is also the movement of electrons from a source, but this transfer is done very quickly and all the electrons move at one time, so little work can be done. To have a current, electrons must flow through the conductor continuously. This happens because of a potential difference which is also called **voltage (V)**. This can happen when there are many extra electrons at one point and a great shortage at the other point. The potential difference is measured in volts. Electric current can be measured in **amperes (A)**. This is the rate of flow of electrons from a source.

Batteries and generators are the two main sources of electric current.

Waves

Water, light, and sound all move in waves. Water waves are easiest to observe, but all three kinds of waves have similar properties. A wave is caused by **vibrations**. A vibration is the back-and-forth movement of particles of matter. **Mechanical waves** are waves that can travel only through matter. Sound waves are this kind of wave. You cannot have a sound wave if you do not have air or water or some other substance to carry the sound.

Electromagnetic waves do not need to travel through matter. Light, microwaves, radio waves, x-rays, and gamma rays are examples of electromagnetic waves.

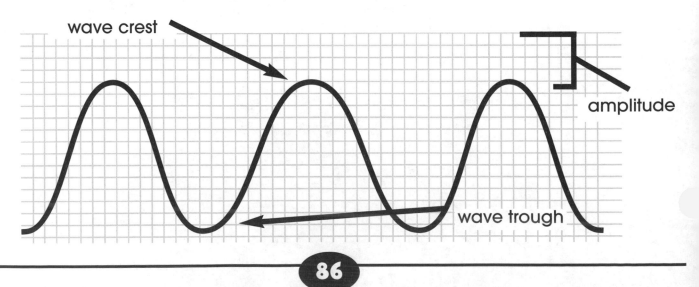

wave crest

amplitude

wave trough

Types of Circuits

Electric Meter

Your house has an **electric meter** that measures the amount of electricity your family uses. The meter measures the electricity in **kilowatt hours**. It would take one kilowatt hour to light ten light bulbs (100 watts each) for one hour.

Circuit

A **circuit** is a path along which electricity travels. It travels in a loop around the circuit. In the circuit pictured below, the electricity travels through the wire, battery, switch and bulb. The electricity must have a source. What is the source in this circuit? You're right if you said the battery.

If the wire in the circuit was cut, there would be a **gap.** The electricity wouldn't be able to flow across the gap. Then, the bulb would not light. This is an example of an **open circuit.** If there were no gaps, the bulb would light. This is an example of a **closed circuit.**

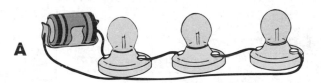

A

B

Series and Parallel Circuits

You can light several light bulbs with only one cell. In picture **A**, the bulbs are connected in a **series circuit.** What would happen to the circuit if you unscrewed one bulb? All the lights would go out. In picture **B**, the bulbs are connected in a **parallel circuit.** What would happen if you unscrewed a light bulb in a parallel circuit? The other lights would still burn.

Dry cells can also be connected in series and parallel circuits. However, cells are usually connected in series. A series of cells increases the amount of power that flows in a circuit. A series of cells will make a light bulb burn brighter.

Conductors and Insulators

The bulb won't light in the circuit pictured here. What's wrong with the circuit? It has a gap. How could you fill the gap to make a closed circuit? The easiest way would be to connect the two wires, but with what?

What would happen if you placed a paper clip across the gap? How about a nail? The bulb would light up. The nail or paper clip would form a bridge across the gap. The nail and paper clip carry, or **conduct**, electricity. They are both **conductors.**

Some materials will not carry the electricity well enough to make the bulb light. Try a rubber band. The bulb won't light. Rubber is a poor conductor of electricity. It is called an **insulator**.

Power Plants

Where does the electricity that is in your house come from? It all begins at a large **power plant.** The power plant has a large **turbine generator.** High-pressure steam spins the turbines and the generator that is attached to the turbine shaft. As the generator spins, it produces hundreds of megawatts of electricity.

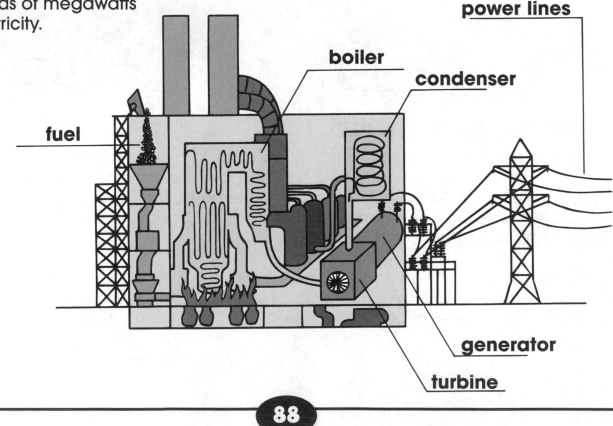

fuel

boiler

condenser

power lines

generator

turbine

Standards of Measurement

United States Conventional System

In many countries, the metric system is the standard of measurement at work, in the laboratory, and at home. In the United States, we use a system of measurement called the United States Conventional System. Our system is based on the British Imperial System of measurement.

Volume

Capacity is the measure of how much liquid a container will hold. The customary units of capacity are **fluid ounce (fl. oz.)**, **cup (c.)**, **pint (pt.)**, **quart (qt.)**, and **gallon (gal.)**.

 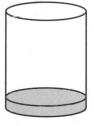 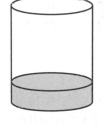 

| 1 c. = 8 oz. | 1 pt. = 2 c. | 1 qt. = 2 pt. | 1 gal. = 4 qt. |

Weight

Weight measures the force of gravity applied to an object. The customary units for weight are the **ounce (oz.)**, **pound (lb.)**, and **ton (tn.)**.

A large strawberry weighs about 1 ounce.

A hardcover book weighs about 1 pound.

A small car weighs about 1 ton.

Distance

The customary units for measuring length are **inch (in.)**, **foot (ft.)**, **yard (yd.)**, and **mile (mi.)**.

A paper clip is about 1 inch long.

A notebook is about 1 foot wide.

A baseball bat is about 1 yard long.

A mile is the distance 4 times around a running track.

Metric System

The metric system was developed by a group of French scientists appointed to a special French National Assembly during the time of the French Revolution. It is a decimal system which makes it easy to convert one unit to another.

Volume

The basic metric unit of capacity is the **liter**. The most common units are the **milliliter (ml)** and **liter (L)**.

A soda cap holds about 1 milliliter.
One liter is a little larger than a quart.

Weight

The basic metric unit of weight is the **gram**. The most common units are the **milligram (mg)**, **gram (g)**, and **kilogram (kg)**.

A short human hair weighs about 1 milligram.

A paper clip weighs about 1 gram.

A textbook weighs about 1 kilogram.

Distance

The basic metric unit of length is the **meter**. The most common units are the **millimeter (mm)**, **centimeter (cm)**, **meter (m)**, and **kilometer (km)**.

This line is 1 millimeter long.　　　　　.

This line is about 1 centimeter long.　━━

A baseball bat is about 1 meter long.

A kilometer is about the distance
2 times around a running track.

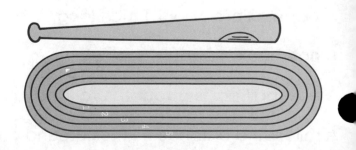

Laboratory Instruments

In the laboratory, you use several tools and instruments that are similar to, but not the same as, items you might have at home. Look at the descriptions on the left and the pictures on the right and match the letters of the items with the correct descriptions.

The balance is used to weigh something. The item being weighed is placed on the balance pan and the weights are added or removed until the pan balances or is level.

Tongs are used to hold hot or extremely cold items or items that cannot be picked up by hand.

A graduated cylinder is sometimes called a graduate. It is a tall, slender cylinder used to measure the volume of liquids.

A ring stand is a tall metal pole on a stand. It is used to hold something off the ground or table.

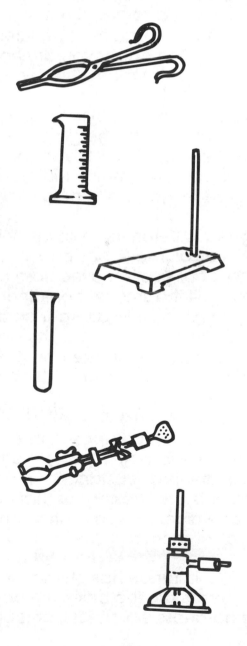

A test tube is used for mixing, heating, cooling, and observing chemicals or other items.

A test tube clamp can be attached to a test tube and then clamped to a ring stand to keep a test tube off of the ground or table.

A Bunsen burner is used to heat chemicals. A Bunsen burner should never be used without adult supervision.

States of Matter

Matter

Three states of matter are commonly known to exist. These are solid, liquid, and gas. The three states of matter will be compared in terms of two characteristics: shape and volume. **Solid** materials are elements or compounds that have definite shapes and definite volumes. A cube of steel has dimensions that do not change regardless of where it is placed, what the pressure outside the cube might be, or how it is oriented. The cube can be sitting on a flat side, teetering on an edge, or balanced on a point, yet it still is the same cube, with the same shape and with the same volume. Solids are what we build with, what we sit upon, and what we walk across. If bridges were not solid, they would squeeze out of the way and our cars would fall through the structures. Walls would run and roofs would collapse and also flow. The paper you are holding would simply disintegrate and spread throughout the room. Bridges, walls, roofs, and paper are all examples of solids.

Liquids have a definite volume, but the shape is not definite. A glass of water fits in the glass whether the glass is tall and thin, short and wide, or in a varying shape. In fact, the water takes the shape of any container in which it is poured. Yet, if it is 100 mL of water, it remains 100 mL of liquid, and only fills the glass to that point. Liquids are used to transmit energy in much the same way.

A **gas** is different from solids or liquids. A gas has no definite shape and it has no definite volume. A gas can fill whatever container in which it is placed. If an amount of gas is moved from a larger to a smaller container, the gas can completely fill the smaller container, fitting into the container at a higher pressure. If the gas is placed into a larger container, the gas completely fills the container, although the pressure of the gas becomes less as the gas spreads into every nook and cranny. The shape and the volume of the gas can change. The gas is capable of doing whatever it takes to fill the container.

Chemical and Physical Properties of Matter

Most matter is composed of a combination of different pure substances. A pure substance is matter that has a fixed composition and distinct properties. For example, water is a substance. It is composed of the elements hydrogen and oxygen. Elements are substances that cannot be broken down into any simpler substances by chemical means. Water can contain many other things—salt (as in seawater), dissolved minerals, and other impurities.

Every substance has physical properties and chemical properties. The physical properties are the color, the odor, the density, the boiling point, the melting point, the hardness or softness, and any other properties that describe the substance.

Mixtures, Solutions, Elements, and Compounds

If two or more substances are combined and each substance stays the same, the combination is called a **mixture**. If the mixture has the same composition and appearance throughout, it is called a **solution**. Salt and pepper stirred together are a mixture. Salt and water stirred together are a solution. In both cases, you can separate the two substances. You can pick the pepper flakes out of the salt, and you can evaporate or boil off the water to leave the salt. An **element** is a substance that cannot be separated into simpler substances by chemical means. A **compound** is a combination of two or more elements which can be separated by chemical means but cannot be separated any other way. An example of a compound is water. Water can be separated into hydrogen and oxygen, which are both elements, but they must be separated by chemical means. You cannot pick the oxygen apart from the hydrogen with tweezers or boil off the hydrogen and leave the oxygen.

Acids

Acids are electrolytes which are able to donate a hydrogen ion when they are dissolved in water. This increases the concentration of H_2. Since a hydrogen ion contains just one proton and one electron, a hydrogen ion is just a single proton with no electron. For this reason, acids are also called proton donors.

Many common substances are acids. Vinegar is acetic acid. Vitamin C is ascorbic acid. To test for acids, you need an acid indicator. One indicator is litmus paper. Litmus paper turns pink when it comes in contact with an acid.

Bases

Bases are also electrolytes. They react with or accept hydrogen ions. Where an acid increases the concentration of hydrogen ions in water, a base increases the concentration of hydroxide or OH ions in water. If the acid and the base are put together, the two ions unite to form water. Soap is a strong base.

Chemical Symbols

When scientists write chemical equations, they do not use the long name for each element. They use an abbreviation of the name called a chemical symbol for each element. For example, oxygen is written as O and hydrogen is written as H.

The periodic table of elements can be found in the Appendices. It lists the atomic number and symbol of every element.

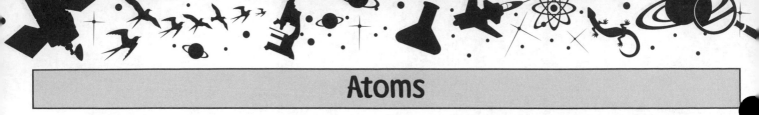

Composition of Atoms

Atoms are composed of three primary particles—**protons**, **neutrons**, and **electrons**. The protons and neutrons share the nucleus, the center of the atom which is the main mass of the atom. The nucleus of the atom is positively charged because protons are positively charged particles and neutrons have no charge. The protons and neutrons are of about equal size. The electrons give the atom its size, but they are tiny, lightweight particles with a negative charge. They orbit the nucleus of the atom.

Protons, electrons, and neutrons are three types of particles found in an atom. The protons and neutrons are found in the nucleus, and the electrons surround the nucleus. The number of protons and electrons will always be the same in a neutral atom.

Atoms of the same element have the same number of protons in the nucleus. Atoms of different elements have a different number of protons in the nucleus. To tell what kind of atom you have, you need to know the number of protons in the nucleus of the atom. This is known as the **atomic number**. The atomic number for the atom below is 6. The mass number is the sum of the protons and neutrons in an atom. Therefore, the mass number for this atom is 12. This atom of carbon is designated C-12. Atoms of an element may have a different number of neutrons in the nucleus. An atom with a different number of neutrons from other atoms of that element is called an **isotope**. The atomic number is given in a subscript that comes in front of the chemical symbol.

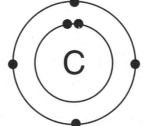

Two or more atoms tightly attached to one another are a **molecule**. These atoms act as a unit, not as separate and distinct kinds of elements. Many elements exist as molecules naturally. Oxygen occurs naturally as two oxygen atoms linked together. The molecular formula of oxygen is written as O^2 and read aloud as "oh-two." The number two in the subscript that follows the chemical symbol shows that each molecule has two atoms. Any molecule that has two atoms is called a **diatomic molecule**. Ozone is another form of oxygen in which the molecules contain three atoms. Both pure oxygen and ozone contain nothing but oxygen, but they have very different chemical and physical properties. O^2 is necessary for animal life while O^3 is poisonous. O^2 has no odor while O^3 has a strong smell.

Chemical Equations and Reactions

Law of Conservation of Mass

In 1789, Antoine Lavoisier, a French nobleman considered to be the father of modern chemistry, wrote what is now called the law of conservation of mass. This scientific law states that "an equal amount of matter exists both before and after the experiment." In other words, in any chemical reaction, matter is neither created nor destroyed. A **chemical reaction** is simply the process by which two or more substances are converted into a third substance. For example, the process of creating water (H_2O) from hydrogen and oxygen is a chemical reaction. To show this chemical reaction, we write a chemical equation. The chemical equation for making water from hydrogen and oxygen is written this way:

$$2H_2 + O_2 \longrightarrow 2H_2O$$

The + sign means "reacts with" or "combines with" and the arrow means "produces." In other words, this equation says that two hydrogen molecules combine with one oxygen molecule to make two molecules of water. The large number before each chemical symbol indicates the number of molecules of the element or compound. Remember that the subscript indicates how many atoms are in one molecule of the element. Both oxygen and hydrogen are diatonic molecules. The equation above shows that there are four atoms of hydrogen and two atoms of oxygen on each side of the arrow. This means that the equations are balanced. A chemical equation cannot have any fractions in it.

A **solution** is a mixture of atoms that is uniform or the same throughout the mixture. An example of a mixture is sugar or $C_{12}H_{22}O_{11}$ dissolved in water.

Concentration is how much of a solute is present in a solution. A concentrated solution is a solution with a fairly large amount of the solute in it.

Chemical reactions are classified as either **ectothermic** or **endothermic**. In ectothermic reactions, heat is produced or passes from the reaction to its surroundings. In endothermic reactions, heat is absorbed from the surroundings.

The rate at which chemicals react can often be increased by adding a **catalyst**. The catalyst controls the rate of the reaction. Sometimes the catalyst remains separate from the chemicals which are being combined, and sometimes the catalyst is also changed in the reaction. The enzymes in your saliva which break foods down into simple sugars are an example of catalysts. The enzymes themselves do not nourish your body or become part of the digested food.

Kinetic and Potential

In scientific terms, **energy** is the ability to do work. Energy exerts the force on the object. You cannot see the energy, but you can see the effects it produces. This energy is always classified as either **kinetic** or **potential**. Kinetic energy is moving energy. A dog running after a ball is demonstrating kinetic energy. Potential energy is energy at rest. It is the ability to do work, energy waiting to be used.

Types of Energy

There are many different forms or kinds of energy. **Mechanical energy** is the energy of motion. Things that are moving or have moving parts have mechanical energy. A person running across a football field has mechanical energy.

Heat or **thermal energy** is the energy that propels a steam engine. Thermal energy is also what pushes the piston in a car.

Electric energy comes from electricity. We harness electricity to run many kinds of compound machines.

Radiant energy is energy which travels in rays. **Solar energy**, or energy from the Sun, is one form of radiant energy. We are trying to develop ways to use more solar energy instead of using chemical energy, nuclear energy, and electrical energy.

Atomic Charge

All atoms contain protons, electrons, and neutrons. The neutrons are heavy and large, but electrically neutral. They do not have a **charge**. Protons have a positive charge but they do not leave the atom. They are in the nucleus and stay with the neutrons. The electrons orbiting the nucleus are the mobile particles.

Electrons can move more easily through some materials than others. Materials which allow the electrons to move easily are called **conductors**. Materials which block the flow of electrons or do not allow the electrons to move easily through them are called **insulators**.

Radiation

Heat, a form of energy, can be transmitted in three different ways. The first way that heat can move is **radiation**. Radiation is how the energy of the Sun reaches Earth through the void of space which separates the Sun and Earth. This special type of wave action delivers heat and light, as well as other forms of energy, from the Sun. Radiation is also how a campfire feels warm to a hand held up to it. There is no physical connection necessary between the hot material and what is being heated. As you stand near a campfire, you do not need to be directly over it, where the heated air rises from the fire, nor do you have to hold something in the fire to bring its warming energy to you. As you get closer to the fire, the heat increases simply due to the waves moving from the fire to you without connection.

Convection

Convection is the movement of heat that is accomplished by the movement of heated material from one place to another. The radiator in a house warms air near the radiator. This air becomes less dense and rises. It is pushed aside by more heated air rising from beneath. The air is pushed across the ceiling and descends on the other side of the room, warming you as you sit on a couch far away from the radiator. You are warmed, not by the radiator directly, but by the air that has traveled to you from where it had been earlier warmed by the radiator.

Conduction

Conduction is the movement of heat through a solid material, as the heat energy is passed from molecule to molecule. This can be seen if one holds a steel rod in a fire. The heat energy is transmitted through the rod from the fire, and the rod becomes hot, clear to the end opposite that which is in the fire. Many campers are familiar with this effect if they use metal marshmallow roasting "sticks." Conduction is why your feet may become uncomfortably hot when walking on pavement in the summer, and it is why you "burn" your hand if you touch a hot container. The heat energy of the hot container is passed directly to your hand. The movement of heat energy through this most direct contact is conduction.

Newton's Three Laws of Motion

Force

Force is the push or pull that one object exerts on another. If you push a book across the table, the power that you use to push that book is **force**. If you pull a shade down on a window, the power that you use is force. Force can affect an object in one of three ways. Force can start the object moving or stop the object from moving. Force can cause the object to move in a different direction. Force can change the speed of the object's movement.

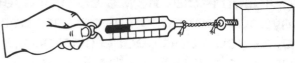

Newton's Three Laws of Motion

All moving objects on Earth are governed by Sir Isaac Newton's three laws of motion. These laws are as follows:

> **1st Law**: Objects at rest stay at rest and objects in motion stay in motion unless acted on by a force.

> **2nd Law**: Acceleration of an object depends on its mass and the size and direction of the force acting on it.

> **3rd Law**: Every action has an equal and opposite reaction force.

Earth's Gravity

Gravity is a force that is explained only in terms of its effects rather than its actual cause. For some reason, objects tend to draw toward one another in direct proportion to their size, and they tend to loose attraction in proportion to the square of the distance that separates them.

The greater the two masses involved actually are, the more gravity is exerted. This explains why your gravitational attraction to the earth is greater than your gravitational attraction to the wall closest to where you are sitting. You are drawn toward the center of the earth, causing a friction that far overcomes your gravitational attraction for the wall. Thus, you sit in a chair and do not go sliding into the nearest wall.

When a force is exerted on you that resists gravity, that force causes you to have weight. The floor, for instance, exists between you and the center of earth's gravity. If you place a scale between you and the floor, the push you have against the scale is measured as your weight. However, if the floor were to vanish, you would begin to fall freely with respect to gravity, and the scale would read zero. This condition, the condition in which gravity acts freely on an object, is called weightlessness. Weightlessness is the condition in which astronauts exist as their space shuttle continually falls toward the earth (gravity is acting freely).

Machines

Machines help to make work like pushing, pulling, and lifting easier. A machine is often made up of different parts that move, is sometimes big and complicated and is other times small and simple.

A **simple machine** is something that changes the direction of the force or the amount of force required to move an object. A **compound machine** is made of two or more simple machines.

Levers

When you use a lever, you can lift a heavy load without pushing very hard. A lever is a bar which may be made out of metal, wood, or other hard material.

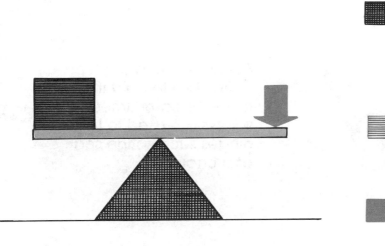

fulcrum—In order for the lever to work, it must rest on a steady object. That object is called the fulcrum.

load—The thing to be moved by the lever is called the load.

force—The push or pull that moves the lever is called the force.

There are three classes of levers—**first-class**, **second-class**, and **third-class**. All levers have a resistance arm, an effort arm, and a fulcrum. Examine the sketches of the three classes of levers below for the positions of the fulcrum, the effort arm, and the resistance arm.

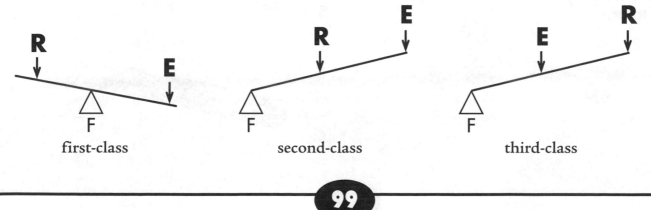

first-class   second-class   third-class

Simple Machines

Here are some examples and definitions of some simple machines.

Lever—A hammer can be used as a kind of lever. This type of machine helps to move things with less force.

Wheel—(such as those on a wagon or car) Wheels can be used to move things more easily from one place to another.

Pulley— A pulley can be used to hoist a flag or sail. Pulleys can be used to lift loads more easily.

Screw—Screws are typically used to hold things together. Sometimes screws are used to lift hinges such as the seat of a chair.

Wedge—An axe is an example of a kind of wedge. Wedges help cut or split things.

Inclined plane—A ramp up to a building is an example of an inclined plane. This type of simple machine can be used to move things from a lower place to a higher place and vice versa.

Gears

Gears are special kinds of wheels that have teeth. If possible, examine the gears of a bicycle. You should note how the large pedal is connected with the small back gear by a chain. Push the pedal to show how the chain makes the small gear in the back work.

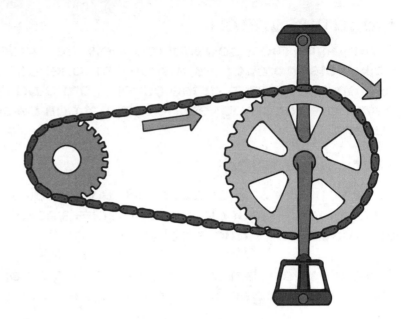

Screw and Wedge

A screw is a special kind of inclined plane. A spiral stairway is also an inclined plane. Two or more inclined planes that are joined together to make a sharp edge or point form a wedge. A **wedge** is a special kind of inclined plane. A wedge is used to pierce or split things. A knife is a wedge.

Wheel and Axle

A doorknob is a simple machine you use every day. It is a **wheel and axle machine**. The wheel is connected to the axle. The axle is a center post. When the wheel moves, the axle does, too.

Opening a door by turning the axle with your fingers is very hard. But by turning the doorknob, which is the "wheel," you use much less force. The doorknob turns the axle for you. The doorknob makes it easy because it is much bigger than the axle. You turn the doorknob a greater distance, but with much less force.

Sometimes the "wheel" of a wheel-and-axle machine doesn't look like a wheel. But look at the path the doorknob makes when it is turned. The path makes a circle, just like a wheel.

Magnets

Electromagnets

Some of the most powerful magnets are made with electricity. These magnets are called **electromagnets**. A strong magnet can be made by winding wire around an iron bar. As soon as the current from a battery is switched on, the bar becomes a strong electromagnet. The magnet can be switched off by stopping the flow of current.

Static Electricity

Have you ever scuffed your feet as you walked across the carpet and then brought your finger close to someone's nose? Zap! Did the person jump? The spark you made was **static electricity.**

Static electricity is made when objects gain or lose tiny bits of electricity called **electrical charges.** The charges are either positive or negative.

Objects that have electrical charges act like magnets, attracting or repelling each other. If two objects have **like charges** (the same kind of charges), they will repel each other. If the two objects have **unlike charges** (different charges), the objects will attract each other.

Magnets and Their Poles

The ends of a magnet are called its **poles.** One pole is called the north-seeking pole or **north pole**; the other is the south-seeking pole, or **south pole**.

When the poles of two bar magnets are put near each other, they have a force that will either pull them together or push them part. If the poles are **different**, then they will pull together, or **attract** each other. (One pole is a south pole and one pole is a north pole.) If the poles are the **same**, then they will push apart, or **repel** each other. (They are either both south poles or both north poles.) The push and pull force of a magnet is called **magnetism.**

The Earth is like a big magnet and has magnetic poles just like a magnet. The Earth's magnetic poles are near the Earth's **true poles.** A **compass** is a free-turning magnet. Compasses that you buy are made with a thin magnet, called a **needle,** that turns freely inside a case. The case is made of a non-magnetic material. The north-seeking pole of the magnet is attracted toward the Earth's **magnetic north pole.** The other end points to the **magnetic south pole.** A compass helps you find the directions north and south.

Magnets/Compass

There is a **compass rose** in the corner of the map below. The compass rose gives the eight compass directions: North (N), South (S), East (E), West (W), Northeast (NE), Southeast (SE), Southwest (SW), and Northwest (NW).

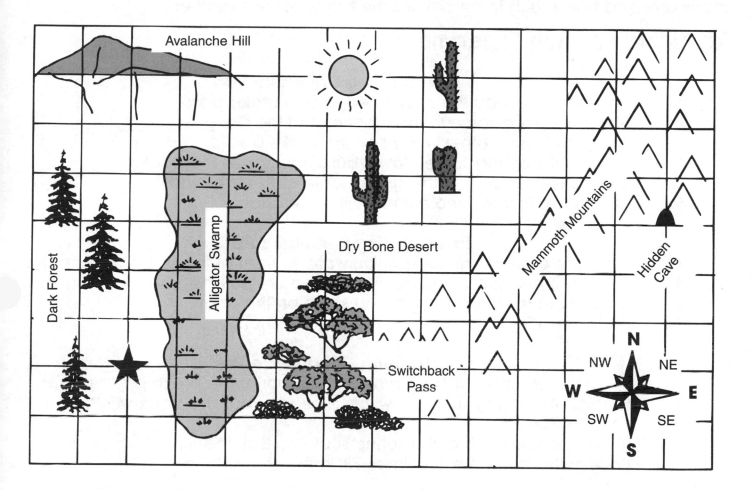

Friction

Friction

Friction is the force that keeps some things from moving or slows them down when they do move. Friction is present when surfaces touch one another. The amount of friction depends on the kinds of materials that are touching, how smooth their surfaces are, and how much force presses the two surfaces together.

Reducing Friction Experiment

Investigating Dry Brake Pad

1. Tie a string around the outside edge of a brake pad.
2. Attach a spring scale to the other end of the string.
3. Place a book or other weight on the brake pad.
4. Holding the spring scale, slowly, but steadily, pull the book.
5. Record the reading of the spring scale as the "dry" trial.
6. Repeat the test two more times. Fill in the chart.

Investigating Wet Brake Pad

7. Reset the equipment but sprinkle water in front of the brake pad's path.
8. Holding the spring scale, slowly, but steadily, pull the book.
9. Record the reading of the spring scale on the chart.
10. Repeat the test two more times. Fill in the chart.

Investigating Oiled Brake Pad

11. Reset the equipment, but sprinkle oil in front of the brake pad's path.
12. Holding the spring scale, slowly, but steadily, pull the book with the spring scale.
13. Record the reading of the spring scale on the chart.
14. Repeat the test two more times. Fill in the chart.

Reading a Spring Scale				
	Trial 1	**Trial 2**	**Trial 3**	**Average**
Dry brake pad				
Wet brake pad				
Oil brake pad				

INVESTIGATION AND EXPERIMENTATION

Scientific Method

The **scientific method** is the way scientists learn and study the world around them. You become a scientist when you try to find answers to your questions by using the scientific method.

Asking questions and coming up with answers is the basis for the scientific method. So, when you begin your science project, you begin with a question that you have. The educated guess you make about this question is called a **hypothesis**.

After you have asked the question and made an educated guess, you have to perform tests to determine whether or not your hypothesis is right. To test your hypothesis, you must follow a **procedure**, which is the name given to the steps you take in your experiment or fieldwork. Your experiment or fieldwork should give you information that can be measured. For instance, if you are trying to determine whether bears are happier in the wild or in the zoo, you must decide how you are going to measure happiness. Perhaps you base a bear's happiness on the amount of food it eats. Putting your information in measurable terms allows you to show **quantitatively** (though numbers) whether your hypothesis is correct or incorrect. It is also important to conduct your test multiple times and use as many test subjects as possible to make sure your results are consistent before you make your conclusion.

Your **conclusion** describes how your **data**, or the results you received from your experiment, compare to your hypothesis. Did your data show that you were right in your educated guess, or did it show that you were wrong? A disproved hypothesis is just as important as a proven hypothesis because it gave important information to others. Your conclusion should also include any new questions that arise as you are doing your experiment. Perhaps when testing whether a bear is happier in the wild or in the zoo, you find that you are not seeing a change in the bear's eating habits, but you do notice they act differently towards other bears. Your new question might be, how does a bear's interaction with other bears change in different environments? What might seem like a failed hypothesis may turn into a new question and an even better experiment.

Planning Your Investigation

Questions:
(Purpose) _____
_____

Materials
Needed: _____
_____
_____
_____

Your
Hypothesis: _____
_____

Steps in Your Procedure

1.

2.

3.

4.

5.

Results: Record observations and/or collect data. (Examples: Keep a log.
Draw diagrams. Make a chart or table.)

Conclusion: _____
_____
_____

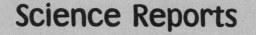

Science Reports

Science reports give information about a subject using description, facts, or examples. Reports explain ideas or facts to the reader. Start by picking a topic that interests you. A science report can be about a scientist, a discovery, an experiment, or a fact.

Once you have chosen a topic, use the library to research that topic. The library catalog is a great source for books, magazine articles, Internet articles, and other resources that have information on your topic. Gather information and take notes. Remember to record the author, title, publisher's information, and page numbers in your notes so that you can write a bibliography.

The most important part of a science report is organizing the information. The information should be easy to read, and it should flow from one idea to another. Organize your research information using one of the following ideas.

Use "order of importance" to explain the causes of the topic (such as allergies), the uses of the topic (such as gold), or a scientist's inventions. Start with the most important fact and then write about the second most important fact, the third most important fact, and then the least important fact.

Use "problem-cause-solution" for topics such as ways to avoid skin cancer, better ways to distribute the world's food, ways to save energy, or ways to solve another problem. Start your paper by describing the problem. In the body of the paper, explain all the causes of the problem. The solution to the problem is the conclusion of the paper.

Write your first draft. When you have finished your draft, reread it carefully. Make sure that it is well organized and makes sense. Remember to proofread the paper. When you have revised and proofread, write out or type a final copy.

APPENDICES

Leaves and Trees

TYPES OF TREES

GYMNOSPERMS are nonflowering trees that bear "naked seeds"—seeds that are not enclosed within an ovary. Many gymnosperms are cone-bearing conifers with needle- or scalelike leaves.

ANGIOSPERMS are flowering trees that bear seeds that are enclosed within an ovary. Broadleaf trees bear fruits such as nuts and berries.

ARRANGEMENT OF LEAVES

NEEDLELEAF

Fascicled

Clustered

BROADLEAF

Alternate

Opposite

Whorled

PARTS OF A TREE

Some trees are deciduous; they shed their leaves each year. Other trees are evergreen; they grow new leaves before shedding old ones.

LEAVES make food for the tree.

CORK, a tree's outer bark, protects the inside of the tree.

PHLOEM, a tree's inner bark, carries food made by the leaves to other parts of the tree.

ROOTS absorb water and nutrients from the soil.

XYLEM consists of two types of wood: sapwood and heartwood.

SAPWOOD, on the outside, carries water from the roots to the leaves.

HEARTWOOD, on the inside, helps support the tree.

CAMBIUM, which lies between the xylem and phloem, promotes the growth of new wood and inner bark.

TYPES OF LEAVES

Simple

Palmately compound

Odd-pinnately compound

Even-pinnately compound

Bipinnately compound

PHOTOSYNTHESIS

A green substance in leaves called chlorophyll captures energy from sunlight, then carries out a process called photosynthesis in which carbon dioxide from the air combines with water from the soil and divides into hydrogen and oxygen. Hydrogen and carbon dioxide combine to form simple sugar. The oxygen is released into the air.

Acacia Deciduous/Angiosperm	**Alder, Red** Deciduous/Angiosperm	**Apple, Common** Deciduous/Angiosperm	**Ash, White** Deciduous/Angiosperm	**Aspen, Quaking** Deciduous/Angiosperm
Basswood Deciduous/Angiosperm	**Bayberry, Southern** Evergreen/Angiosperm	**Beech, American** Deciduous/Angiosperm	**Birch, Paper** Deciduous/Angiosperm	**Boxelder** Deciduous/Angiosperm
Chokecherry, Common Deciduous/Angiosperm	**Cottonwood** Deciduous/Angiosperm	**Dogwood** Deciduous/Angiosperm	**Douglas-fir** Evergreen/Gymnosperm	**Elm, American** Deciduous/Angiosperm
Hackberry Deciduous/Angiosperm	**Hawthorn, Scarlet** Deciduous/Angiosperm	**Hemlock** Evergreen/Gymnosperm	**Hickory, Shagbark** Deciduous/Angiosperm	**Holly, American** Evergreen/Angiosperm

Leaves and Trees

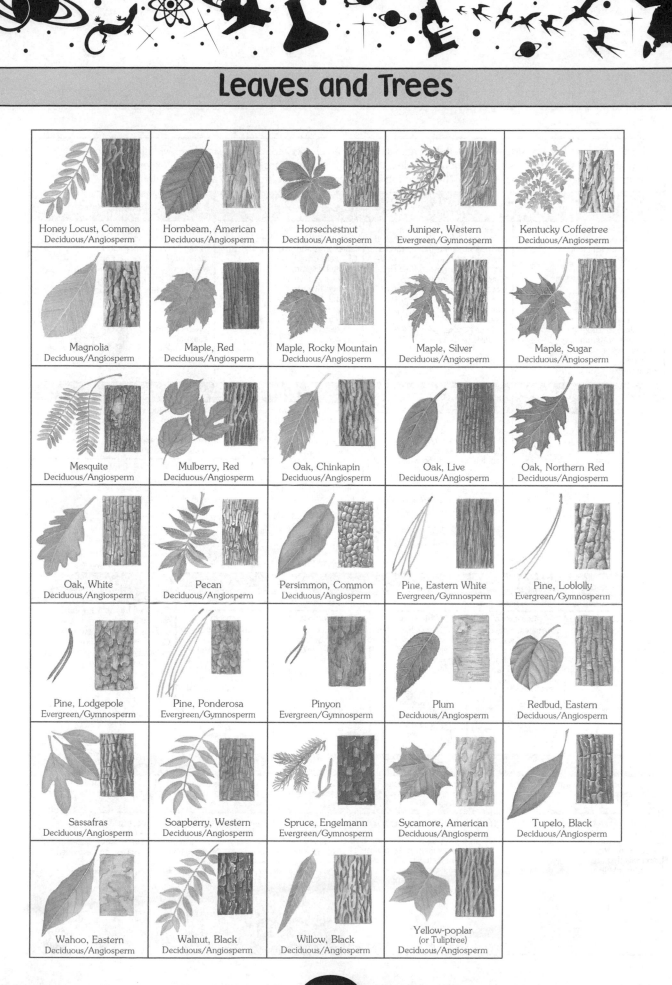

Honey Locust, Common Deciduous/Angiosperm	Hornbeam, American Deciduous/Angiosperm	Horsechestnut Deciduous/Angiosperm	Juniper, Western Evergreen/Gymnosperm	Kentucky Coffeetree Deciduous/Angiosperm
Magnolia Deciduous/Angiosperm	Maple, Red Deciduous/Angiosperm	Maple, Rocky Mountain Deciduous/Angiosperm	Maple, Silver Deciduous/Angiosperm	Maple, Sugar Deciduous/Angiosperm
Mesquite Deciduous/Angiosperm	Mulberry, Red Deciduous/Angiosperm	Oak, Chinkapin Deciduous/Angiosperm	Oak, Live Deciduous/Angiosperm	Oak, Northern Red Deciduous/Angiosperm
Oak, White Deciduous/Angiosperm	Pecan Deciduous/Angiosperm	Persimmon, Common Deciduous/Angiosperm	Pine, Eastern White Evergreen/Gymnosperm	Pine, Loblolly Evergreen/Gymnosperm
Pine, Lodgepole Evergreen/Gymnosperm	Pine, Ponderosa Evergreen/Gymnosperm	Pinyon Evergreen/Gymnosperm	Plum Deciduous/Angiosperm	Redbud, Eastern Deciduous/Angiosperm
Sassafras Deciduous/Angiosperm	Soapberry, Western Deciduous/Angiosperm	Spruce, Engelmann Evergreen/Gymnosperm	Sycamore, American Deciduous/Angiosperm	Tupelo, Black Deciduous/Angiosperm
Wahoo, Eastern Deciduous/Angiosperm	Walnut, Black Deciduous/Angiosperm	Willow, Black Deciduous/Angiosperm	Yellow-poplar (or Tuliptree) Deciduous/Angiosperm	

Animal Kingdom

The animal kingdom consists of multicellular organisms that feed by ingestion. On the simplest level, they are made up of tissues. As the animals become more complex, these tissues form organs. At the most complex level, these tissues and organs form organ systems. The following is an overview of a portion of the animal kingdom.

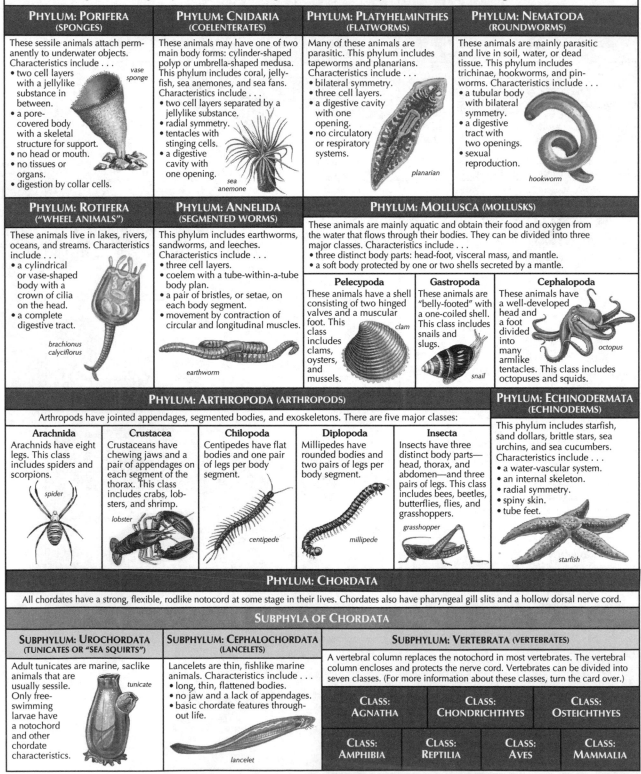

PHYLUM: PORIFERA (SPONGES)

These sessile animals attach permanently to underwater objects. Characteristics include . . .
- two cell layers with a jellylike substance in between.
- a pore-covered body with a skeletal structure for support.
- no head or mouth.
- no tissues or organs.
- digestion by collar cells.

vase sponge

PHYLUM: CNIDARIA (COELENTERATES)

These animals may have one of two main body forms: cylinder-shaped polyp or umbrella-shaped medusa. This phylum includes coral, jellyfish, sea anemones, and sea fans. Characteristics include . . .
- two cell layers separated by a jellylike substance.
- radial symmetry.
- tentacles with stinging cells.
- a digestive cavity with one opening.

sea anemone

PHYLUM: PLATYHELMINTHES (FLATWORMS)

Many of these animals are parasitic. This phylum includes tapeworms and planarians. Characteristics include . . .
- bilateral symmetry.
- three cell layers.
- a digestive cavity with one opening.
- no circulatory or respiratory systems.

planarian

PHYLUM: NEMATODA (ROUNDWORMS)

These animals are mainly parasitic and live in soil, water, or dead tissue. This phylum includes trichinae, hookworms, and pinworms. Characteristics include . . .
- a tubular body with bilateral symmetry.
- a digestive tract with two openings.
- sexual reproduction.

hookworm

PHYLUM: ROTIFERA ("WHEEL ANIMALS")

These animals live in lakes, rivers, oceans, and streams. Characteristics include . . .
- a cylindrical or vase-shaped body with a crown of cilia on the head.
- a complete digestive tract.

brachionus calyciflorus

PHYLUM: ANNELIDA (SEGMENTED WORMS)

This phylum includes earthworms, sandworms, and leeches. Characteristics include . . .
- three cell layers.
- coelem with a tube-within-a-tube body plan.
- a pair of bristles, or setae, on each body segment.
- movement by contraction of circular and longitudinal muscles.

earthworm

PHYLUM: MOLLUSCA (MOLLUSKS)

These animals are mainly aquatic and obtain their food and oxygen from the water that flows through their bodies. They can be divided into three major classes. Characteristics include . . .
- three distinct body parts: head-foot, visceral mass, and mantle.
- a soft body protected by one or two shells secreted by a mantle.

Pelecypoda
These animals have a shell consisting of two hinged valves and a muscular foot. This class includes clams, oysters, and mussels.

clam

Gastropoda
These animals are "belly-footed" with a one-coiled shell. This class includes snails and slugs.

snail

Cephalopoda
These animals have a well-developed head and a foot divided into many armlike tentacles. This class includes octopuses and squids.

octopus

PHYLUM: ARTHROPODA (ARTHROPODS)

Arthropods have jointed appendages, segmented bodies, and exoskeletons. There are five major classes:

Arachnida
Arachnids have eight legs. This class includes spiders and scorpions.

spider

Crustacea
Crustaceans have chewing jaws and a pair of appendages on each segment of the thorax. This class includes crabs, lobsters, and shrimp.

lobster

Chilopoda
Centipedes have flat bodies and one pair of legs per body segment.

centipede

Diplopoda
Millipedes have rounded bodies and two pairs of legs per body segment.

millipede

Insecta
Insects have three distinct body parts—head, thorax, and abdomen—and three pairs of legs. This class includes bees, beetles, butterflies, flies, and grasshoppers.

grasshopper

PHYLUM: ECHINODERMATA (ECHINODERMS)

This phylum includes starfish, sand dollars, brittle stars, sea urchins, and sea cucumbers. Characteristics include . . .
- a water-vascular system.
- an internal skeleton.
- radial symmetry.
- spiny skin.
- tube feet.

starfish

PHYLUM: CHORDATA

All chordates have a strong, flexible, rodlike notocord at some stage in their lives. Chordates also have pharyngeal gill slits and a hollow dorsal nerve cord.

SUBPHYLA OF CHORDATA

SUBPHYLUM: UROCHORDATA (TUNICATES OR "SEA SQUIRTS")

Adult tunicates are marine, saclike animals that are usually sessile. Only free-swimming larvae have a notochord and other chordate characteristics.

tunicate

SUBPHYLUM: CEPHALOCHORDATA (LANCELETS)

Lancelets are thin, fishlike marine animals. Characteristics include . . .
- long, thin, flattened bodies.
- no jaw and a lack of appendages.
- basic chordate features throughout life.

lancelet

SUBPHYLUM: VERTEBRATA (VERTEBRATES)

A vertebral column replaces the notochord in most vertebrates. The vertebral column encloses and protects the nerve cord. Vertebrates can be divided into seven classes. (For more information about these classes, turn the card over.)

CLASS: AGNATHA	CLASS: CHONDRICHTHYES		CLASS: OSTEICHTHYES
CLASS: AMPHIBIA	CLASS: REPTILIA	CLASS: AVES	CLASS: MAMMALIA

Animal Kingdom

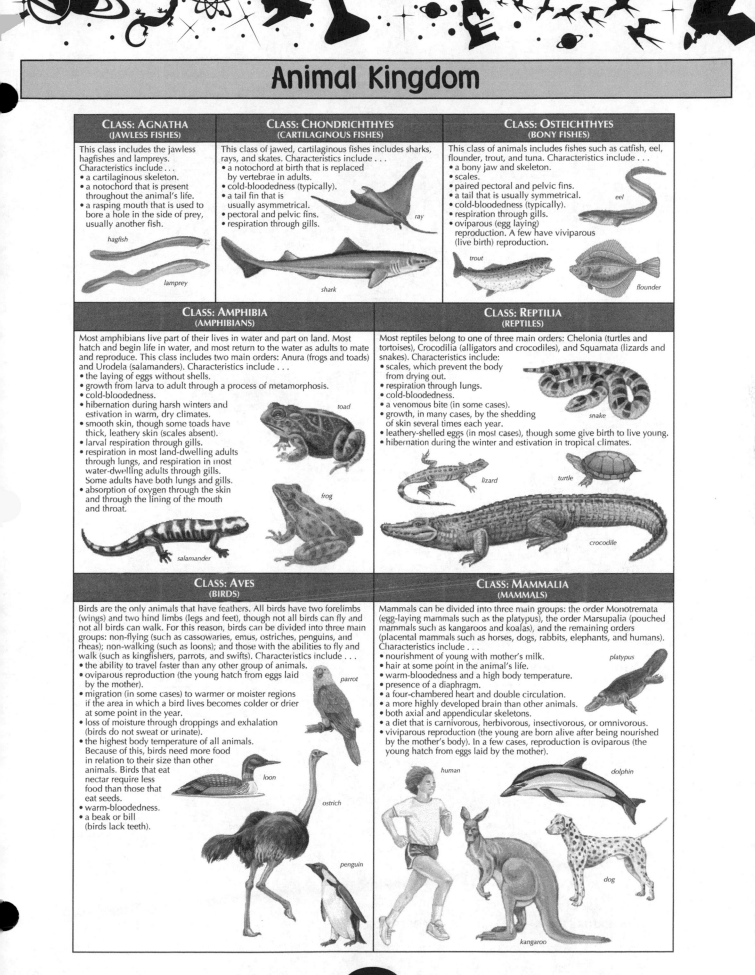

CLASS: AGNATHA
(JAWLESS FISHES)

This class includes the jawless hagfishes and lampreys. Characteristics include . . .
- a cartilaginous skeleton.
- a notochord that is present throughout the animal's life.
- a rasping mouth that is used to bore a hole in the side of prey, usually another fish.

hagfish

lamprey

CLASS: CHONDRICHTHYES
(CARTILAGINOUS FISHES)

This class of jawed, cartilaginous fishes includes sharks, rays, and skates. Characteristics include . . .
- a notochord at birth that is replaced by vertebrae in adults.
- cold-bloodedness (typically).
- a tail fin that is usually asymmetrical.
- pectoral and pelvic fins.
- respiration through gills.

ray

shark

CLASS: OSTEICHTHYES
(BONY FISHES)

This class of animals includes fishes such as catfish, eel, flounder, trout, and tuna. Characteristics include . . .
- a bony jaw and skeleton.
- scales.
- paired pectoral and pelvic fins.
- a tail that is usually symmetrical.
- cold-bloodedness (typically).
- respiration through gills.
- oviparous (egg laying) reproduction. A few have viviparous (live birth) reproduction.

eel

trout

flounder

CLASS: AMPHIBIA
(AMPHIBIANS)

Most amphibians live part of their lives in water and part on land. Most hatch and begin life in water, and most return to the water as adults to mate and reproduce. This class includes two main orders: Anura (frogs and toads) and Urodela (salamanders). Characteristics include . . .
- the laying of eggs without shells.
- growth from larva to adult through a process of metamorphosis.
- cold-bloodedness.
- hibernation during harsh winters and estivation in warm, dry climates.
- smooth skin, though some toads have thick, leathery skin (scales absent).
- larval respiration through gills.
- respiration in most land-dwelling adults through lungs, and respiration in most water-dwelling adults through gills. Some adults have both lungs and gills.
- absorption of oxygen through the skin and through the lining of the mouth and throat.

toad

frog

salamander

CLASS: REPTILIA
(REPTILES)

Most reptiles belong to one of three main orders: Chelonia (turtles and tortoises), Crocodilia (alligators and crocodiles), and Squamata (lizards and snakes). Characteristics include:
- scales, which prevent the body from drying out.
- respiration through lungs.
- cold-bloodedness.
- a venomous bite (in some cases).
- growth, in many cases, by the shedding of skin several times each year.
- leathery-shelled eggs (in most cases), though some give birth to live young.
- hibernation during the winter and estivation in tropical climates.

snake

lizard

turtle

crocodile

CLASS: AVES
(BIRDS)

Birds are the only animals that have feathers. All birds have two forelimbs (wings) and two hind limbs (legs and feet), though not all birds can fly and not all birds can walk. For this reason, birds can be divided into three main groups: non-flying (such as cassowaries, emus, ostriches, penguins, and rheas); non-walking (such as loons); and those with the abilities to fly and walk (such as kingfishers, parrots, and swifts). Characteristics include . . .
- the ability to travel faster than any other group of animals.
- oviparous reproduction (the young hatch from eggs laid by the mother).
- migration (in some cases) to warmer or moister regions if the area in which a bird lives becomes colder or drier at some point in the year.
- loss of moisture through droppings and exhalation (birds do not sweat or urinate).
- the highest body temperature of all animals. Because of this, birds need more food in relation to their size than other animals. Birds that eat nectar require less food than those that eat seeds.
- warm-bloodedness.
- a beak or bill (birds lack teeth).

parrot

loon

ostrich

penguin

CLASS: MAMMALIA
(MAMMALS)

Mammals can be divided into three main groups: the order Monotremata (egg-laying mammals such as the platypus), the order Marsupialia (pouched mammals such as kangaroos and koalas), and the remaining orders (placental mammals such as horses, dogs, rabbits, elephants, and humans). Characteristics include . . .
- nourishment of young with mother's milk.
- hair at some point in the animal's life.
- warm-bloodedness and a high body temperature.
- presence of a diaphragm.
- a four-chambered heart and double circulation.
- a more highly developed brain than other animals.
- both axial and appendicular skeletons.
- a diet that is carnivorous, herbivorous, insectivorous, or omnivorous.
- viviparous reproduction (the young are born alive after being nourished by the mother's body). In a few cases, reproduction is oviparous (the young hatch from eggs laid by the mother).

platypus

human

dolphin

kangaroo

dog

Skeletal System

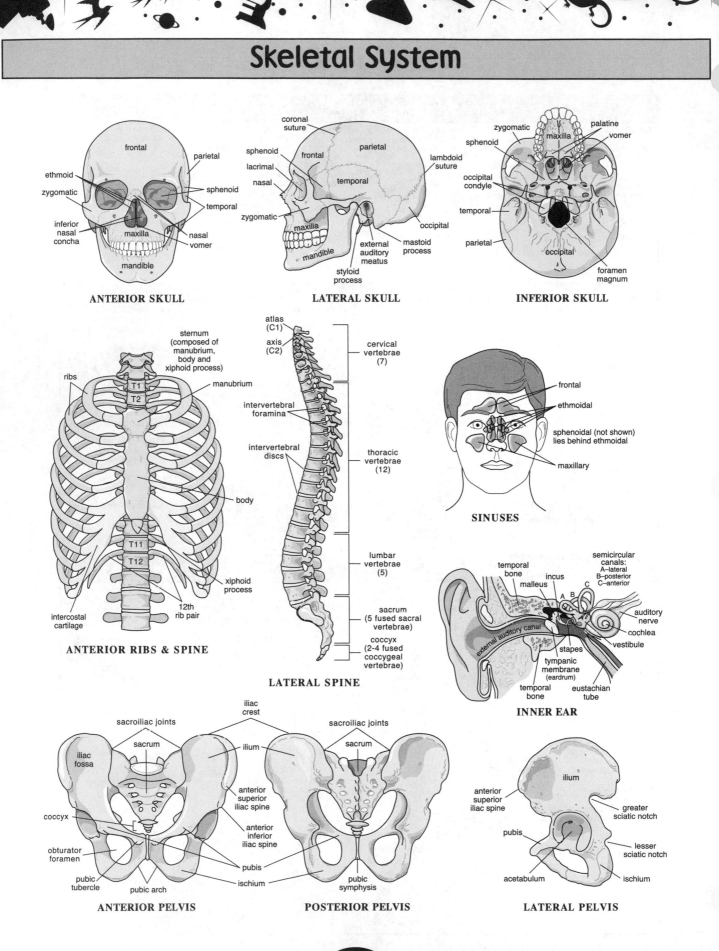

ANTERIOR SKULL

frontal
parietal
ethmoid
sphenoid
zygomatic
temporal
inferior
nasal
concha
maxilla
nasal
vomer
mandible

LATERAL SKULL

coronal
suture
sphenoid
lacrimal
nasal
zygomatic
frontal
parietal
lambdoid
suture
temporal
maxilla
mandible
occipital
external
auditory
meatus
mastoid
process
styloid
process

INFERIOR SKULL

zygomatic
palatine
maxilla
vomer
sphenoid
occipital
condyle
temporal
parietal
occipital
foramen
magnum

ANTERIOR RIBS & SPINE

sternum
(composed of
manubrium,
body and
xiphoid process)
ribs
T1
T2
manubrium
body
T11
T12
xiphoid
process
intercostal
cartilage
12th
rib pair

LATERAL SPINE

atlas
(C1)
axis
(C2)
cervical
vertebrae
(7)
intervertebral
foramina
intervertebral
discs
thoracic
vertebrae
(12)
lumbar
vertebrae
(5)
sacrum
(5 fused sacral
vertebrae)
coccyx
(2-4 fused
coccygeal
vertebrae)

SINUSES

frontal
ethmoidal
sphenoidal (not shown)
lies behind ethmoidal
maxillary

INNER EAR

semicircular
canals:
A–lateral
B–posterior
C–anterior
temporal
bone
incus
malleus
A B C
auditory
nerve
cochlea
vestibule
external auditory canal
stapes
tympanic
membrane
(eardrum)
temporal
bone
eustachian
tube

ANTERIOR PELVIS

sacroiliac joints
sacrum
iliac
crest
ilium
iliac
fossa
anterior
superior
iliac spine
anterior
inferior
iliac spine
coccyx
obturator
foramen
pubis
ischium
pubic
tubercle
pubic arch

POSTERIOR PELVIS

sacroiliac joints
sacrum
pubic
symphysis

LATERAL PELVIS

ilium
anterior
superior
iliac spine
greater
sciatic notch
pubis
lesser
sciatic notch
acetabulum
ischium

Skeletal System

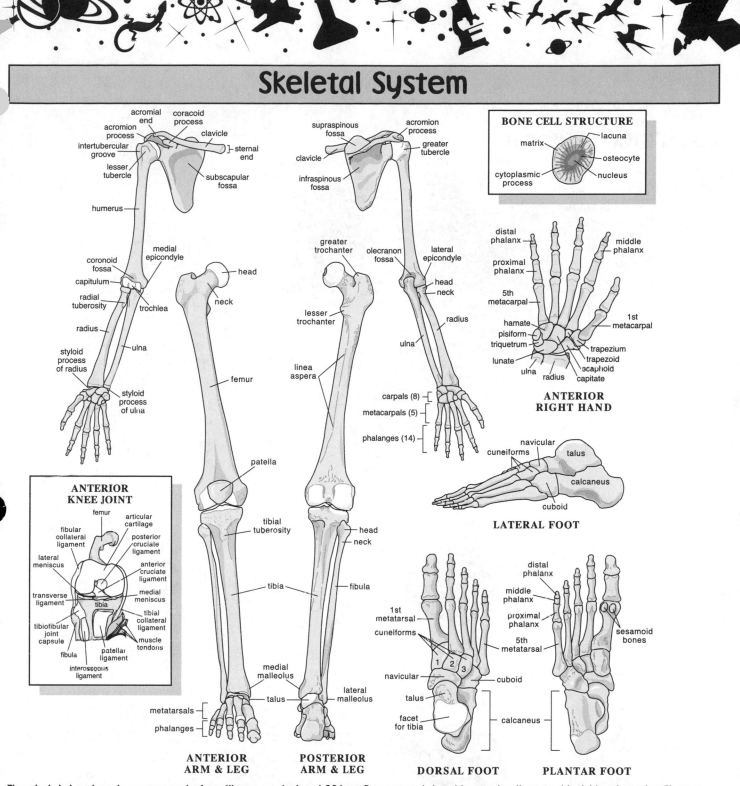

BONE CELL STRUCTURE
- matrix
- lacuna
- cytoplasmic process
- osteocyte
- nucleus

ANTERIOR RIGHT HAND

LATERAL FOOT

ANTERIOR KNEE JOINT

ANTERIOR ARM & LEG

POSTERIOR ARM & LEG

DORSAL FOOT

PLANTAR FOOT

The skeletal system is composed of cartilage and about 206 separate bones. The skeletal system supports the body, protects vital organs (such as the brain, heart, and lungs), provides a site for muscle attachment and works with the muscular system to enable movement. The bones store calcium and phosphorus along with trace amounts of magnesium, potassium, and sodium. Red marrow, a tissue that produces red blood cells, is found in flat bones such as the skull, ribs, and sternum. Yellow marrow, a fat-storage tissue, is usually found in the cavity of a long bone.

The human body is composed of the axial and appendicular skeletons. The axial skeleton includes the skull, vertebral column, sternum, and ribs. The appendicular skeleton includes the arms, legs, and the pectoral and pelvic girdles.

Bones are joined to each other and held in place by fibrous connective tissue called ligaments. The point at which two or more bones meet is called a joint. The following are the types of joints:

A. Immovable (i.e., cranial bones)

B. Slightly movable (i.e., vertebral bones)

C. Freely movable–two bones separated by a cavity
1. Hinge–allows movement in one direction only (i.e., at elbow and knee)
2. Ball-and-socket–allows for rotational movement and movement along all planes (i.e., hips)

Body Systems

Circulatory System

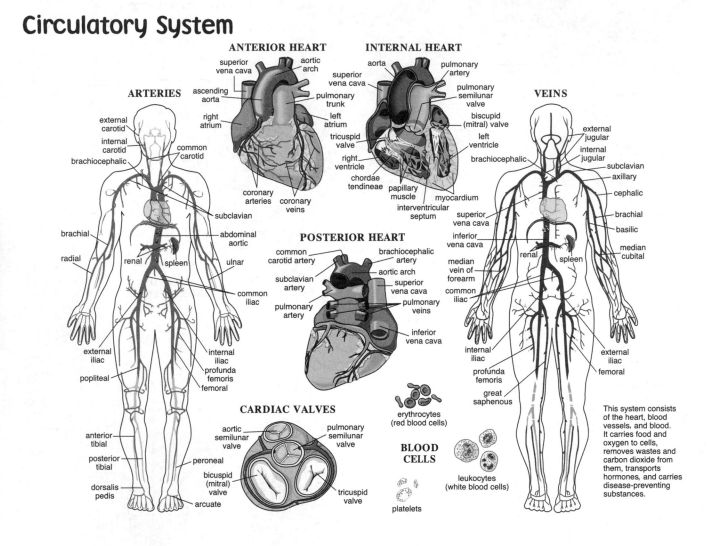

ANTERIOR HEART

superior vena cava
aortic arch
ascending aorta
right atrium
pulmonary trunk
left atrium
tricuspid valve
right ventricle
chordae tendineae
coronary arteries
coronary veins

INTERNAL HEART

aorta
pulmonary artery
superior vena cava
pulmonary semilunar valve
biscupid (mitral) valve
left ventricle
right ventricle
papillary muscle
myocardium
interventricular septum

ARTERIES

external carotid
internal carotid
brachiocephalic
common carotid
brachial
radial
renal
spleen
subclavian
abdominal aortic
ulnar
common iliac
external iliac
popliteal
internal iliac
profunda femoris
femoral
anterior tibial
posterior tibial
peroneal
bicuspid (mitral) valve
dorsalis pedis
tricuspid valve
arcuate

POSTERIOR HEART

common carotid artery
brachiocephalic artery
subclavian artery
aortic arch
superior vena cava
pulmonary artery
pulmonary veins
inferior vena cava

CARDIAC VALVES

aortic semilunar valve
pulmonary semilunar valve
bicuspid (mitral) valve
tricuspid valve

VEINS

external jugular
internal jugular
subclavian
axillary
cephalic
brachial
basilic
median cubital
brachiocephalic
superior vena cava
inferior vena cava
median vein of forearm
common iliac
renal
spleen
internal iliac
profunda femoris
great saphenous
external iliac
femoral

erythrocytes (red blood cells)

BLOOD CELLS

leukocytes (white blood cells)

platelets

This system consists of the heart, blood vessels, and blood. It carries food and oxygen to cells, removes wastes and carbon dioxide from them, transports hormones, and carries disease-preventing substances.

Digestive System

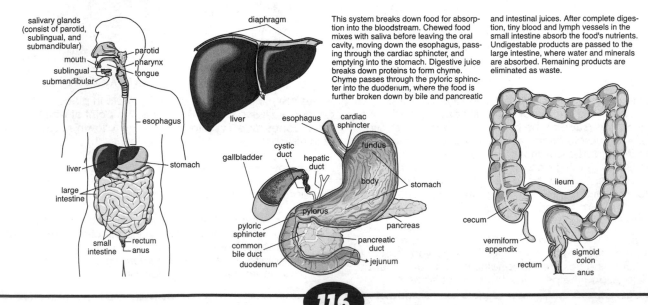

salivary glands (consist of parotid, sublingual, and submandibular)
mouth
sublingual
submandibular
parotid
pharynx
tongue
esophagus
liver
stomach
large intestine
small intestine
rectum
anus

diaphragm
liver

This system breaks down food for absorption into the bloodstream. Chewed food mixes with saliva before leaving the oral cavity, moving down the esophagus, passing through the cardiac sphincter, and emptying into the stomach. Digestive juice breaks down proteins to form chyme. Chyme passes through the pyloric sphincter into the duodenum, where the food is further broken down by bile and pancreatic and intestinal juices. After complete digestion, tiny blood and lymph vessels in the small intestine absorb the food's nutrients. Undigestable products are passed to the large intestine, where water and minerals are absorbed. Remaining products are eliminated as waste.

esophagus
cardiac sphincter
cystic duct
gallbladder
hepatic duct
fundus
body
stomach
pyloric sphincter
common bile duct
duodenum
pylorus
pancreas
pancreatic duct
jejunum

ileum
cecum
vermiform appendix
sigmoid colon
rectum
anus

Body Systems

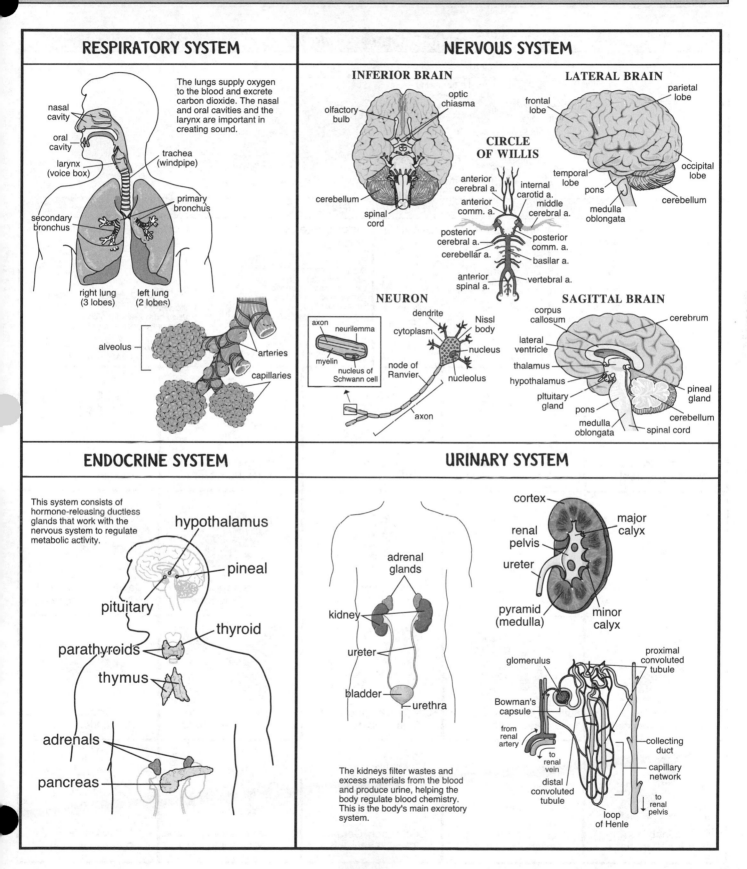

RESPIRATORY SYSTEM

The lungs supply oxygen to the blood and excrete carbon dioxide. The nasal and oral cavities and the larynx are important in creating sound.

- nasal cavity
- oral cavity
- larynx (voice box)
- trachea (windpipe)
- primary bronchus
- secondary bronchus
- right lung (3 lobes)
- left lung (2 lobes)
- alveolus
- arteries
- capillaries

NERVOUS SYSTEM

INFERIOR BRAIN
- olfactory bulb
- optic chiasma
- cerebellum
- spinal cord

LATERAL BRAIN
- frontal lobe
- parietal lobe
- temporal lobe
- occipital lobe
- pons
- cerebellum
- medulla oblongata

CIRCLE OF WILLIS
- anterior cerebral a.
- anterior comm. a.
- internal carotid a.
- middle cerebral a.
- posterior cerebral a.
- posterior comm. a.
- cerebellar a.
- basilar a.
- anterior spinal a.
- vertebral a.

NEURON
- axon
- neurilemma
- myelin
- nucleus of Schwann cell
- dendrite
- cytoplasm
- Nissl body
- nucleus
- node of Ranvier
- nucleolus
- axon

SAGITTAL BRAIN
- corpus callosum
- cerebrum
- lateral ventricle
- thalamus
- hypothalamus
- pituitary gland
- pineal gland
- pons
- cerebellum
- medulla oblongata
- spinal cord

ENDOCRINE SYSTEM

This system consists of hormone-releasing ductless glands that work with the nervous system to regulate metabolic activity.

- hypothalamus
- pineal
- pituitary
- thyroid
- parathyroids
- thymus
- adrenals
- pancreas

URINARY SYSTEM

- adrenal glands
- kidney
- ureter
- bladder
- urethra

- cortex
- major calyx
- renal pelvis
- ureter
- pyramid (medulla)
- minor calyx

The kidneys filter wastes and excess materials from the blood and produce urine, helping the body regulate blood chemistry. This is the body's main excretory system.

- glomerulus
- proximal convoluted tubule
- Bowman's capsule
- from renal artery
- to renal vein
- distal convoluted tubule
- loop of Henle
- collecting duct
- capillary network
- to renal pelvis

Insects

External Anatomy of an Insect

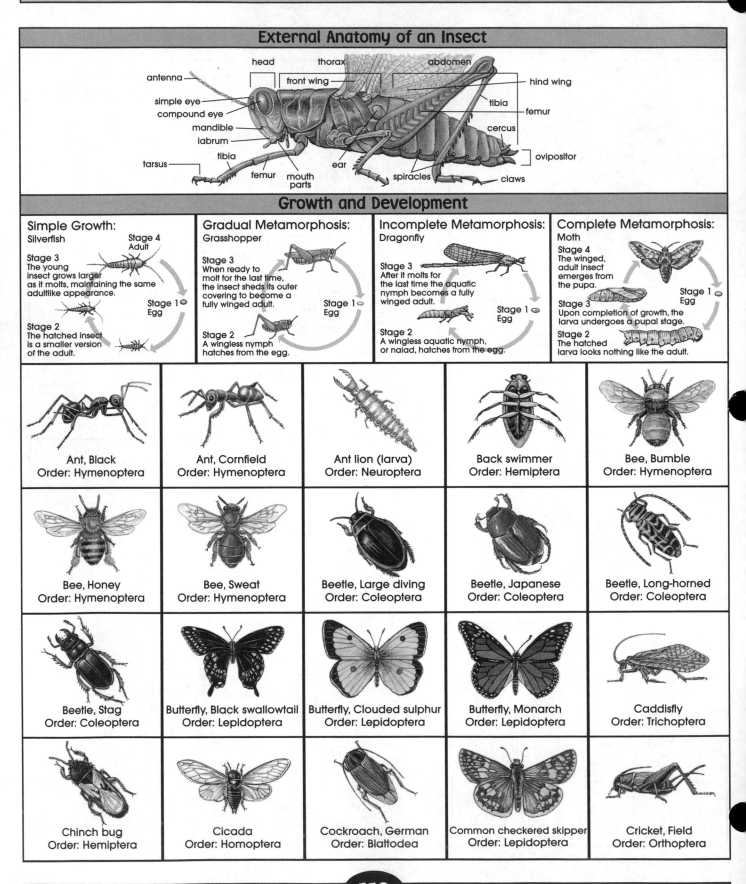

antenna
head
thorax
abdomen
front wing
hind wing
simple eye
compound eye
tibia
mandible
femur
labrum
cercus
tibia
tarsus
femur
mouth parts
ear
spiracles
ovipositor
claws

Growth and Development

Simple Growth:
Silverfish

Stage 4
Adult

Stage 3
The young insect grows larger as it molts, maintaining the same adultlike appearance.

Stage 1
Egg

Stage 2
The hatched insect is a smaller version of the adult.

Gradual Metamorphosis:
Grasshopper

Stage 3
When ready to molt for the last time, the insect sheds its outer covering to become a fully winged adult.

Stage 1
Egg

Stage 2
A wingless nymph hatches from the egg.

Incomplete Metamorphosis:
Dragonfly

Stage 3
After it molts for the last time the aquatic nymph becomes a fully winged adult.

Stage 1
Egg

Stage 2
A wingless aquatic nymph, or naiad, hatches from the egg.

Complete Metamorphosis:
Moth

Stage 4
The winged, adult insect emerges from the pupa.

Stage 1
Egg

Stage 3
Upon completion of growth, the larva undergoes a pupal stage.

Stage 2
The hatched larva looks nothing like the adult.

Ant, Black Order: Hymenoptera	Ant, Cornfield Order: Hymenoptera	Ant lion (larva) Order: Neuroptera	Back swimmer Order: Hemiptera	Bee, Bumble Order: Hymenoptera
Bee, Honey Order: Hymenoptera	Bee, Sweat Order: Hymenoptera	Beetle, Large diving Order: Coleoptera	Beetle, Japanese Order: Coleoptera	Beetle, Long-horned Order: Coleoptera
Beetle, Stag Order: Coleoptera	Butterfly, Black swallowtail Order: Lepidoptera	Butterfly, Clouded sulphur Order: Lepidoptera	Butterfly, Monarch Order: Lepidoptera	Caddisfly Order: Trichoptera
Chinch bug Order: Hemiptera	Cicada Order: Homoptera	Cockroach, German Order: Blattodea	Common checkered skipper Order: Lepidoptera	Cricket, Field Order: Orthoptera

Insects

Cricket, House Order: Orthoptera	**Damsel fly, Black-winged** Order: Odonata	**Darner, Green** Order: Odonata	**Dragonfly, Ten-spot** Order: Odonata	**Earwig** Order: Dermaptera
Fly, House Order: Diptera	**Fly, Crane** Order: Diptera	**Fly, Horse** Order: Diptera	**Grasshopper, Short, horned** Order: Orthoptera	**Harlequin bug or Stink bug** Order: Hemiptera
Hornet Baldfaced Order: Hymenoptera	**Junebug** (a.k.a. June Beetle or May beetle) Order: Coleoptera	**Katydid, Northern (true)** Order: Orthoptera	**Lacewig Goldeneyed** Order: Neuroptera	**Ladybug or Lady beetle** Order: Coleoptera
Leafhopper Order: Homoptera	**Lightning bug or Firefly** Order: Coleoptera	**Mantid Carolina** (a.k.a. Praying mantis) Order: Mantodea	**Mayfly** Order: Ephemeroptera	**Mosquito** Order: Diptera
Moth, Isabella tiger Order: Lepidoptera	**Moth, Gypsy** Order: Lepidoptera	**Silverfish** Order: Thysanura	**Springtail** Order: Collembola	**Squash bug** Order: Hemiptera
Stonefly Order: Plecoptera	**Termite, Subterranean** Order: Isoptera	**Treehopper, Buffalo** Order: Homoptera	**Walkingstick** Order: Phasmatodea	**Wasp, Ichneumon** Order: Hymenoptera
Water bug, Giant Order: Hemiptera	**Water strider** Order: Hemiptera	**Weevil, Acorn** Order: Coleoptera	**Yellow jacket** Order: Hymenoptera	

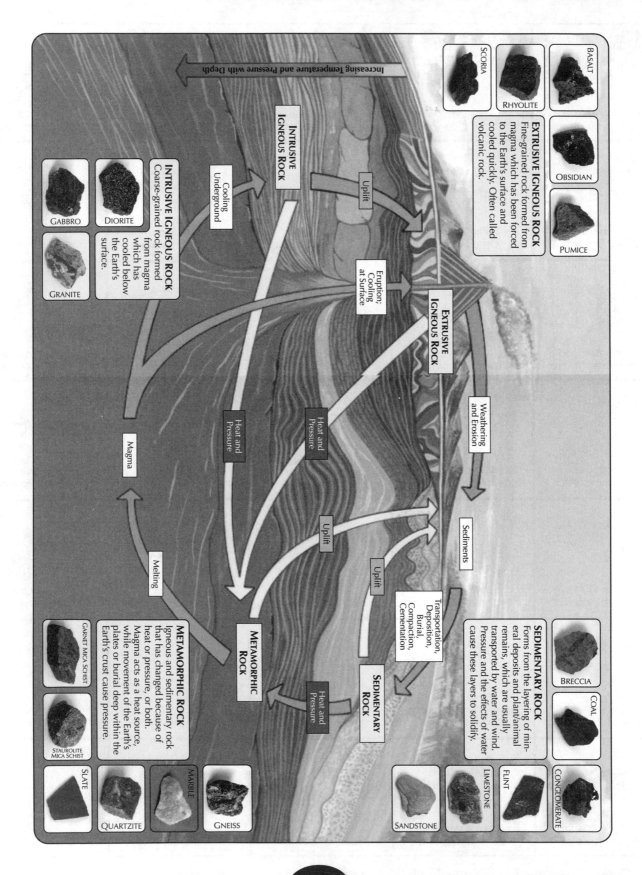

Increasing Temperature and Pressure with Depth

INTRUSIVE IGNEOUS ROCK

INTRUSIVE IGNEOUS ROCK
Coarse-grained rock formed from magma which has cooled below the Earth's surface.

GABBRO

DIORITE

GRANITE

Cooling Underground

Eruption; Cooling at Surface

EXTRUSIVE IGNEOUS ROCK

EXTRUSIVE IGNEOUS ROCK
Fine-grained rock has been formed from magma which has been forced to the Earth's surface and cooled quickly. Often called volcanic rock.

SCORIA

RHYOLITE

BASALT

OBSIDIAN

PUMICE

Uplift

Weathering and Erosion

Heat and Pressure

Heat and Pressure

Magma

Melting

Uplift

Uplift

Sediments

Transportation, Deposition, Burial, Compaction, Cementation

METAMORPHIC ROCK

METAMORPHIC ROCK
Igneous and sedimentary rock that has changed because of heat or pressure, or both. Magma acts as a heat source, while movement of the Earth's plates or burial deep within the Earth's crust cause pressure.

GARNET MICA SCHIST

STAUROLITE MICA SCHIST

SLATE

QUARTZITE

MARBLE

GNEISS

Heat and Pressure

SEDIMENTARY ROCK

SEDIMENTARY ROCK
Forms from the layering of mineral deposits and plant/animal remains, which are usually transported by water and wind. Pressure and the effects of water cause these layers to solidify.

BRECCIA

COAL

CONGLOMERATE

FLINT

LIMESTONE

SANDSTONE

Rocks and Minerals

ROCKS & MINERALS

Minerals are the basic materials of which all rocks are composed. Minerals can be identified by their physical properties. These properties include hardness, color and streak, cleavage, and luster.

A mineral's hardness can be determined with the Mohs scale. Using specific tools and minerals with known hardness levels, an unidentified mineral can be categorized. This test, along with others, aids in mineral identification.

MOHS HARDNESS SCALE

HARDNESS	MINERAL	COMMON TESTS
1	Talc	Fingernail will scratch it.
2	Gypsum	
3	Calcite	A copper coin will scratch it.
4	Fluorite	Glass or a penknife will scratch it.
5	Apatite	
6	Feldspar or Orthoclase	Will scratch glass.
7	Quartz	
8	Beryl or Topaz	
9	Corundum	Will scratch all common materials.
10*	Diamond	

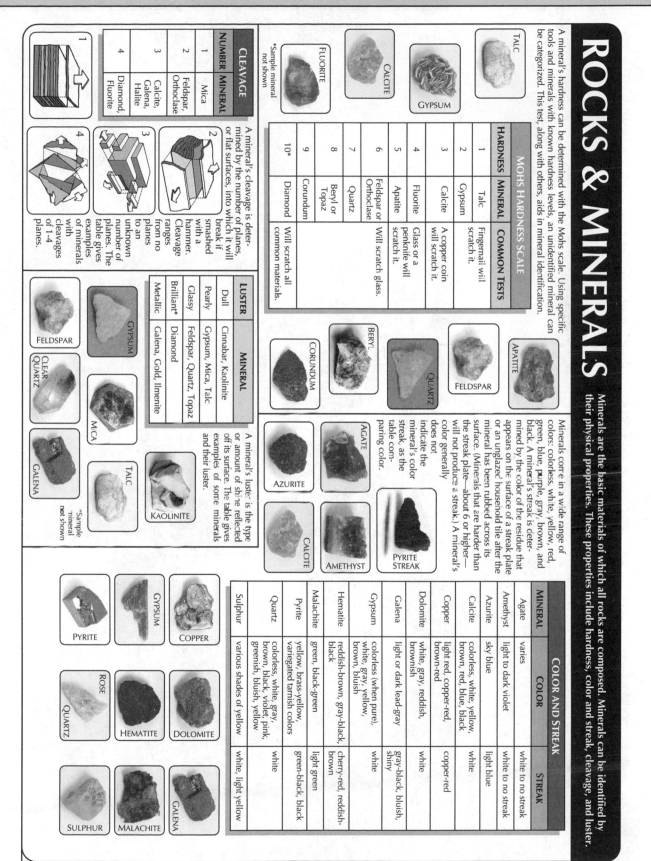

TALC

GYPSUM

CALCITE

FLUORITE

*Sample mineral not shown

CLEAVAGE

NUMBER	MINERAL
1	Mica
2	Feldspar, Orthoclase
3	Calcite, Galena, Halite
4	Diamond, Fluorite

A mineral's cleavage is determined by the number of planes, or flat surfaces, into which it will break if smashed with a hammer. Cleavage ranges from no planes to an unknown number of planes. The table gives examples of minerals with cleavages of 1-4 planes.

Minerals come in a wide range of colors: colorless, white, yellow, red, green, blue, purple, gray, brown, and black. A mineral's streak is determined by the color of the residue that appears on the surface of a streak plate or an unglazed household tile after the mineral has been rubbed across its surface. (Minerals that are harder than the streak plate—about 6 or higher—will not produce a streak.) A mineral's color generally does not indicate the mineral's color streak, as the table comparing color.

LUSTER

LUSTER	MINERAL
Dull	Cinnabar, Kaolinite
Pearly	Gypsum, Mica, Talc
Glassy	Feldspar, Quartz, Topaz
Brilliant*	Diamond
Metallic	Galena, Gold, Ilmenite

A mineral's luster is the type or amount of shine reflected off its surface. The table gives examples of some minerals and their luster.

FELDSPAR · GYPSUM · CLEAR QUARTZ · MICA · GALENA · TALC · KAOLINITE

*Sample mineral not shown

APATITE · FELDSPAR · QUARTZ · BERYL · CORUNDUM · AGATE · AZURITE · AMETHYST · CALCITE · PYRITE STREAK

COLOR AND STREAK

MINERAL	COLOR	STREAK
Agate	varies	white to no streak
Amethyst	light to dark violet	white to no streak
Azurite	sky blue	light blue
Calcite	colorless, white, yellow, brown, red, blue, black	white
Copper	light red, copper-red, brown-red	copper-red
Dolomite	white, gray, reddish, brownish	white
Galena	light or dark lead-gray	gray-black, bluish, shiny
Gypsum	colorless (when pure), white, gray, yellow, brown, bluish	white
Hematite	reddish-brown, gray-black, black	cherry-red, reddish-brown
Malachite	green, black-green	light green
Pyrite	yellow, brass-yellow, variegated tarnish colors	green-black, black
Quartz	colorless, white, gray, brown, black, violet, pink, greenish, bluish, yellow	white
Sulphur	various shades of yellow	white, light yellow

PYRITE · GYPSUM · COPPER · ROSE QUARTZ · HEMATITE · DOLOMITE · SULPHUR · MALACHITE · GALENA

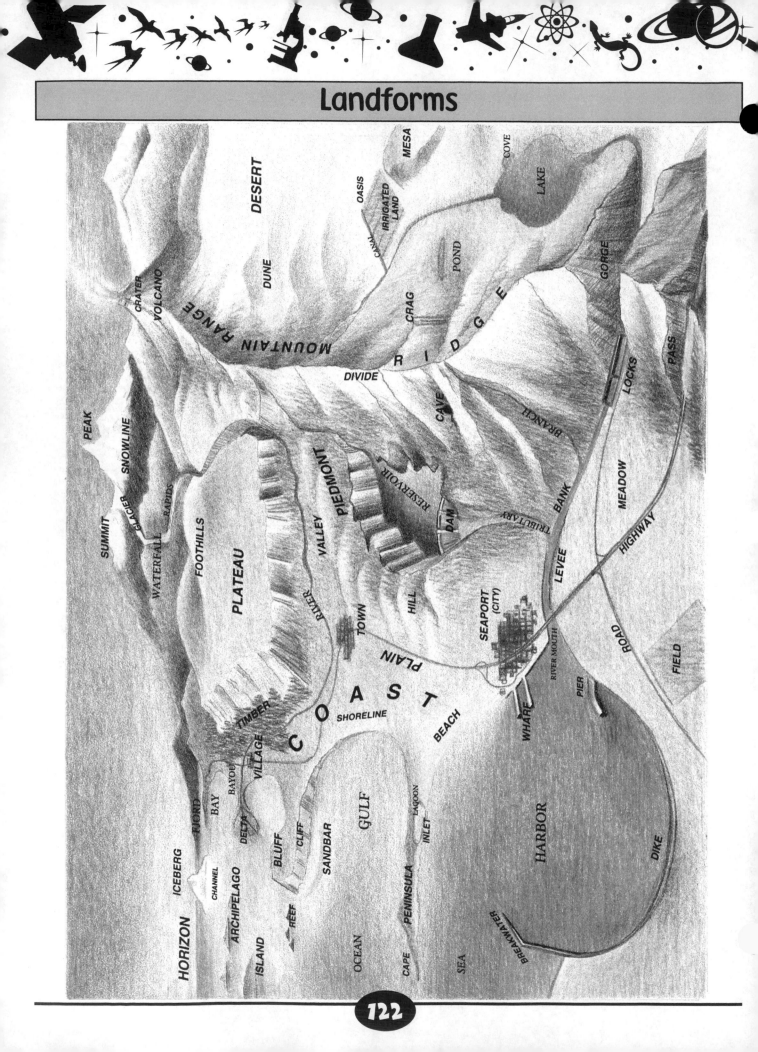

Landforms

ARCHIPELAGO - A large group or chain of islands; also a large area of water containing several islands.

BANK - The border of any stream.

BAY - Any inlet of an ocean, sea, or lake that extends into the land. A bay is smaller than a gulf.

BAYOU - A slow, sluggish stream that meanders through lowlands and marshes.

BEACH - The shore of an ocean or a lake that is covered by sand or pebbles.

BLUFF - A steep bank beside a body of water.

BRANCH - A small stream or creek emptying into a larger stream.

BREAKWATER - A wall built in water near the shore to break the force of the waves and to provide shelter for boats and ships.

CANAL - A constructed channel filled with water used for navigation, irrigation, or drainage.

CAPE - A narrow piece of land projecting into the sea.

CAVE - A deep, hollowed-out area under the earth's surface.

CHANNEL - 1. A narrow strip of water. 2. The deeper part of a stream or body of water which is navigable.

CITY - A larger municipality, usually having a larger population than a town, village, or borough.

CLIFF - The steep, rocky face of a bluff.

COAST - Land along the ocean.

COVE - A small, sheltered bay in the shoreline of any body of water.

CRAG - A projecting point of rock, usually perpendicular.

CRATER - The bowl-shaped opening at the top of a volcano.

DAM - A wall built across a river to hold back flowing water.

DELTA - A deposit of sand, silt, and pebbles that forms at the mouth of a river.

DESERT - A large area of land with little or no moisture or vegetation.

DIKE - Earth or other material built up along a river or ocean to keep the water from overflowing onto the land.

DIVIDE - A watershed; a ridge of land.

DUNE - A hill or ridge of sand heaped up by the wind.

FIELD - A large area of cleared land, often cultivated.

FJORD - A deep, narrow inlet of the sea, between high, rocky banks.

FOOTHILLS - A hilly area at the base of a mountain.

GLACIER - A large sheet of ice, usually at high elevations, which moves slowly over land or down a valley.

GORGE - A narrow passage between steep mountains or hills; a steep, rocky ravine.

GULF - Water bordering on, and laying within, a curved coastline; usually larger than a bay and smaller than a sea; sometimes nearly surrounded by land.

HARBOR - A sheltered body of water where ships anchor and are protected from storms.

HIGHWAY - Main road or thoroughfare.

HILL - A raised landform, not as high as a mountain.

HORIZON - The line where the earth's surface and the sky seem to meet.

ICEBERG - A massive block of floating ice broken away from a glacier.

INLET - A recess, such as a bay, along a coast.

IRRIGATED LAND - Land watered by artificial means through the use of small canals or ditches.

ISLAND - A body of land completely surrounded by water.

LAGOON - 1. A shallow body of water connected to the sea by an inlet. 2. Water enclosed by a narrow strip of land.

LAKE - A body of water completely surrounded by land.

LEVEE - An embankment beside a stream that prevents overflow.

LOCKS - An enclosure with gates built in a canal or river so that ships can be raised or lowered by changing the water level.

MEADOW - An area of level land where grass is grown and usually cut for hay.

MESA - A flat-topped, rocky hill with steeply sloping sides.

MOUNTAIN RANGE - A chain of connecting mountains.

OASIS - A fertile spot in a desert watered by underground springs or by irrigation.

OCEAN - Any one of the four largest connecting bodies of salt water on the earth's surface; the Atlantic, Pacific, Indian, and Arctic Oceans.

PASS - An opening through hills or mountains used as a route for highways or railroads.

PEAK - The pointed top of a mountain.

PENINSULA - A piece of land nearly surrounded by water and attached to a larger area of land or the mainland.

PIEDMONT - An area of rolling land along the foot of a mountain range.

PIER - A structure projecting into the water and used as a docking or loading place for ships.

PLAIN - A large, level area of land.

PLATEAU - A high, flat landform with steep sides. A plateau is larger than a mesa.

POND - A body of water smaller than a lake.

RAPIDS - Part of a stream where the water flows very swiftly over rocks.

REEF - A ridge of rocks or coral in a body of water, which lies slightly beneath, or at, the surface.

RESERVOIR - A natural or artificial lake used to store water.

RIDGE - A long, narrow, conspicuous elevation of land.

RIVER - A large stream of water that drains an area of land and flows into another river or body of water.

RIVER MOUTH - The point where a river empties and ends its course.

ROAD - An open passageway on which vehicles travel.

SANDBAR - A long, narrow bank of sand in a body of water.

SEA - 1. Another word for ocean. 2. A large body of salt water.

SEAPORT - A harbor or town having facilities to load and unload seagoing vessels.

SHORELINE - The edge of a body of water.

SNOWLINE - The line on a mountain above which there is snow year round.

SUMMIT - Highest part of a hill or mountain.

TIMBER - Wooded land covered by trees and used as a source of wood.

TOWN - A large village.

TRIBUTARY - A stream or river that flows into another stream or river.

VALLEY - An area of land between hills or mountains.

VILLAGE - A small group of houses; smaller than a town.

VOLCANO - 1. A cone-shaped mountain formed by lava and cinders that erupted through a crater. 2. An opening in the earth's surface from which molten rock, steam, cinders, gas, and rock fragments are released.

WATERFALL - A flow of water falling from a high place to a low place.

WHARF - A large dock from which ships may load or unload.

Weather

Weather develops in the troposphere, the atmosphere's lowest layer. This is the only layer in which living things can breathe.
All weather conditions develop from the elements of air pressure, moisture, temperature, and wind.

CLOUDS

- Masses of small water droplets or tiny ice crystals that float in the air.
- The three main types are cirrus, cumulus, and stratus. Other clouds are a mixture of these three main types.

Cirrus
- Cirro—means "curled" or "feathery."
- Form highest in the sky; are made up of ice crystals; and appear as curls, tufts, or wisps.
- Usually signal the end of clear weather.

Cumulus
- Cumulo—means "heaped" or "piled."
- Cottony clouds with flat, usually gray bases, and puffy, bright white tops.
- Usually signal good weather, but if atmosphere is unstable, can build into towering clouds that produce showers and thunderstorms.

Stratus
- Strato—means "layerlike" or "sheetlike."
- Low-lying, dull-colored clouds that form in layers or sheets.
- Usually bring drizzling rain or light-falling snow.

Alto
- A prefix meaning "middle range of clouds" and used to describe clouds that lie from 6,500–18,000 ft. (1,980–5,640 m).

Nimbus:
- A rain cloud.

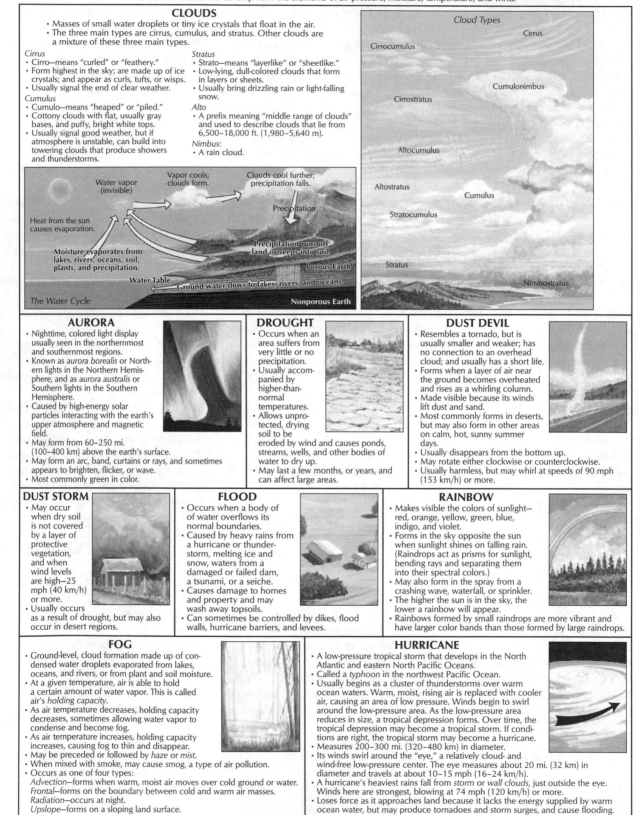

Cloud Types

Cirrus, Cirrocumulus, Cirrostratus, Cumulonimbus, Altocumulus, Altostratus, Cumulus, Stratocumulus, Stratus, Nimbostratus

The Water Cycle:
Water vapor (invisible) · Vapor cools; clouds form. · Clouds cool further; precipitation falls. · Precipitation · Heat from the sun causes evaporation. · Moisture evaporates from lakes, rivers, oceans, soil, plants, and precipitation. · Precipitation runs off land or seeps into soil. · Porous Earth · Water Table · Ground water flows to lakes, rivers, and oceans. · Nonporous Earth

AURORA

- Nighttime, colored light display usually seen in the northernmost and southernmost regions.
- Known as *aurora borealis* or Northern lights in the Northern Hemisphere, and as *aurora australis* or Southern lights in the Southern Hemisphere.
- Caused by high-energy solar particles interacting with the earth's upper atmosphere and magnetic field.
- May form from 60–250 mi. (100–400 km) above the earth's surface.
- May form an arc, band, curtains or rays, and sometimes appears to brighten, flicker, or wave.
- Most commonly green in color.

DROUGHT

- Occurs when an area suffers from very little or no precipitation.
- Usually accompanied by higher-than-normal temperatures.
- Allows unprotected, drying soil to be eroded by wind and causes ponds, streams, wells, and other bodies of water to dry up.
- May last a few months, or years, and can affect large areas.

DUST DEVIL

- Resembles a tornado, but is usually smaller and weaker; has no connection to an overhead cloud; and usually has a short life.
- Forms when a layer of air near the ground becomes overheated and rises as a whirling column.
- Made visible because its winds lift dust and sand.
- Most commonly forms in deserts, but may also form in other areas on calm, hot, sunny summer days.
- Usually disappears from the bottom up.
- May rotate either clockwise or counterclockwise.
- Usually harmless, but may whirl at speeds of 90 mph (153 km/h) or more.

DUST STORM

- May occur when dry soil is not covered by a layer of protective vegetation, and when wind levels are high—25 mph (40 km/h) or more.
- Usually occurs as a result of drought, but may also occur in desert regions.

FLOOD

- Occurs when a body of of water overflows its normal boundaries.
- Caused by heavy rains from a hurricane or thunderstorm, melting ice and snow, waters from a damaged or failed dam, a tsunami, or a seiche.
- Causes damage to homes and property and may wash away topsoils.
- Can sometimes be controlled by dikes, flood walls, hurricane barriers, and levees.

RAINBOW

- Makes visible the colors of sunlight—red, orange, yellow, green, blue, indigo, and violet.
- Forms in the sky opposite the sun when sunlight shines on falling rain. (Raindrops act as prisms for sunlight, bending rays and separating them into their spectral colors.)
- May also form in the spray from a crashing wave, waterfall, or sprinkler.
- The higher the sun is in the sky, the lower a rainbow will appear.
- Rainbows formed by small raindrops are more vibrant and have larger color bands than those formed by large raindrops.

FOG

- Ground-level, cloud formation made up of condensed water droplets evaporated from lakes, oceans, and rivers, or from plant and soil moisture.
- At a given temperature, air is able to hold a certain amount of water vapor. This is called air's *holding capacity*.
- As air temperature decreases, holding capacity decreases, sometimes allowing water vapor to condense and become fog.
- As air temperature increases, holding capacity increases, causing fog to thin and disappear.
- May be preceded or followed by *haze* or *mist*.
- When mixed with smoke, may cause *smog*, a type of air pollution.
- Occurs as one of four types:
  Advection—forms when warm, moist air moves over cold ground or water.
  Frontal—forms on the boundary between cold and warm air masses.
  Radiation—occurs at night.
  Upslope—forms on a sloping land surface.

HURRICANE

- A low-pressure tropical storm that develops in the North Atlantic and eastern North Pacific Oceans.
- Called a *typhoon* in the northwest Pacific Ocean.
- Usually begins as a cluster of thunderstorms over warm ocean waters. Warm, moist, rising air is replaced with cooler air, causing an area of low pressure. Winds begin to swirl around the low-pressure area. As the low-pressure area reduces in size, a tropical depression forms. Over time, the tropical depression may become a tropical storm. If conditions are right, the tropical storm may become a hurricane.
- Measures 200–300 mi. (320–480 km) in diameter.
- Its winds swirl around the "eye," a relatively cloud- and wind-free low-pressure center. The eye measures about 20 mi. (32 km) in diameter and travels at about 10–15 mph (16–24 km/h).
- A hurricane's heaviest rains fall from *storm* or *wall clouds*, just outside the eye. Winds here are strongest, blowing at 74 mph (120 km/h) or more.
- Loses force as it approaches land because it lacks the energy supplied by warm ocean water, but may produce tornadoes and storm surges, and cause flooding.

Weather

LIGHTNING & THUNDER

Lightning:
- A giant electrical spark that occurs during a thunderstorm.
- Develops when large numbers of oppositely charged particles in cumulonimbus clouds flow rapidly toward one another.
- May appear as a bead, branch, chain, fork, ribbon, sheet, or streak.
- Cloud-to-ground or ground-to-cloud lightning may stretch 9 mi. (14 km), while cloud-to-cloud lightning may stretch more than 90 mi. (140 km).

Thunder:
- As lightning flashes, it rapidly heats the surrounding air—often by more than 50,000°F (27,760°C)—and forces it to expand. When the heated air expands, it crashes into cool air and creates the air wave, or sound, known as thunder.
- Because sound travels slower than light, thunder will be heard after lightning flashes, unless the lightning is overhead.

Note: The number of seconds that pass between a lightning flash and the sound of thunder can be used to calculate storm movement. Divide the number of seconds by five for distance in miles and by three for distance in kilometers.

WIND & AIR PRESSURE

- Defined as the circulation of air from a high-pressure area to a low-pressure area.
- The greater the temperature difference between high- and low-pressure areas, the greater the wind speed.
- A wind is named for its speed or for the direction from which it blows.
- May have a specific name if it is common to a certain region (e.g. chinook, monsoon, sirocco, etc.).
- Also named for its general pattern of circulation. (See diagram.)

Fronts:
- Large air masses form over areas where the temperature is fairly constant. When a cold air mass and a warm air mass meet, a front, or area of rapidly changing weather, occurs.
- Fronts are largely responsible for changes in weather—cold fronts cause sudden changes while warm fronts cause more gradual changes.

Doldrums:
- An area of calms, light breezes, and squalls.
- One of the world's rainiest regions.
- Sailing ships often get stuck here from lack of wind.

Trade winds:
- Strong polar winds that blow toward the equator from about 30°N and 30°S latitude.

Horse latitudes:
- An area of light rainfall.
- Many of the world's deserts lie in these areas.
- Sailing ships often get stuck here from lack of wind.

Prevailing westerlies:
- Unsteady winds that blow west to east over the North and South middle latitudes.
- Often interrupted by mountain ranges or cyclonic storms.

Polar easterlies:
- Blow from the poles to about 60°N and 60°S latitude, typically from east to west.

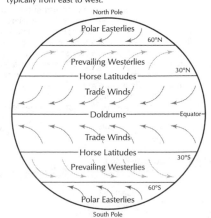

North Pole
Polar Easterlies
60°N
Prevailing Westerlies
30°N
Horse Latitudes
Trade Winds
Doldrums — Equator
Trade Winds
Horse Latitudes
30°S
Prevailing Westerlies
60°S
Polar Easterlies
South Pole

TORNADO & WATERSPOUT

tornado

Tornado:
- One of the smallest, yet most violent, storm types.
- Its winds swirl at speeds of up to 300 mph (480 km/h) or more.
- May be strong enough to uproot trees, overturn railroad cars, lift and transport automobiles, or destroy steel buildings.
- Associated with severe thunderstorms. If conditions are right, a central, low-pressure area develops and winds begin to swirl inward. As winds swirl, a funnel cloud develops. A funnel cloud may remain in the clouds, or touch down to form a tornado.
- Made visible by the condensed water vapor, dirt, and debris raised by its swirling winds.
- Usually funnel-shaped, but may also appear as a thin, twisting rope or as a mass of traveling dark clouds at or near the ground.
- May measure 30 ft.–1.5 mi. (9 m–2.4 km) in diameter.
- May live from a few minutes to several hours.
- May travel a distance of 1–200 mi. (1.6–320 km) or more, at speeds of 10–60 mph (16–97 km/h) or more.
- Sometimes referred to as a *cyclone* or a *twister*.
- Called a *waterspout* if it forms over a lake or ocean.

waterspout

Waterspout:
- A rotating column of air that forms over a warm body of water, most commonly in the tropics.
- Begins as a localized low-pressure center that causes winds to whirl around it. Develops further as a rotating column of air is lifted from the water's surface.
- Usually measures 20–200 ft. (6–60 m) in diameter and is made visible as water vapor condenses in the column and surface water is drawn into the column's base.
- May be called a *tornado* if it moves onto land.

TEMPERATURE

- The amount of internal energy an object has as a result of heating or cooling.
- Measured with a thermometer, usually using the Fahrenheit (°F) or Celsius (°C) temperature scales.
- The earth gets its heat energy from the sun. When the heat enters the earth's atmosphere, about half of it escapes back into space, while the rest is absorbed by the ground and bodies of water. The absorbed heat warms the air.
- Heat affects the amount of water vapor in air. That is why the percentage of humidity can make the atmosphere feel hotter or cooler than the temperature suggests.
- Dew may form on grass, leaves, and cars when ground-level air cools and can no longer hold all of its water vapor. The water vapor then condenses, or becomes liquid.
- If the air temperature drops below 32°F (0°C), water's freezing point, water vapor may turn into ice crystals, or frost.

To find °C when °F is known:
$$°C = (°F - 32)/1.8$$

To find °F when °C is known:
$$°F = °C \times 1.8 + 32$$

PRECIPITATION

- When the droplets or ice crystals within clouds become too heavy for air to hold, they fall to the earth as a form of precipitation, such as snow, sleet, rain, snow pellets, or hail.
- Ice crystals form if a cloud's temperature is below freezing, or less than 32°F (0°C). The ice crystals take on different forms as they fall, depending on the ground-level air temperature.
- *Snow*—falls when the ground-level air temperature is about 37°F (2.78°C).
- *Sleet*—may fall when the ground-level air temperature is about 37–39°F (2.78–3.89°C).
- *Rain*—falls from water-droplet clouds, or when the ground-level air temperature is over 39°F (3.89°C).
- *Snow pellets*—an ice crystal may collide with super-cooled water droplets as it falls. The ice crystal will reach the earth as white pellets called snow pellets, or *graupel*.
- *Hail*—an ice crystal may be carried by strong winds throughout a thundercloud's many layers. The ice crystal will collide with supercooled water pellets, refreeze, and increase in size. When the ice crystal becomes too heavy for air to hold, it will fall to the earth as a hailstone.

WEATHER MAP SYMBOLS

▨	Rain
✱✱✱	Snow
(H)	High pressure
(L)	Low pressure
▶	Wind direction
75/60	High & low daily temperatures (°F)
○	Clear skies
◑	Partly cloudy skies
●	Cloudy skies
▬▲▬	Warm front
▬▲▬	Cold front
▬▲▼▬	Stationary front
▬▲▲▬	Occluded front

WEATHER TOOLS

Name	Measures
Anemometer	Wind speed
Barometer	Air pressure
Hygrometer	Humidity
Rain gauge	Rain level
Thermometer	Temperature
Weather vane	Wind direction
Windsock	Wind direction and strength

Planets

The names of the planets (from nearest the sun to farthest) are Mercury, Venus, Earth, Mars, Jupiter, Saturn, Uranus, Neptune, and Pluto.

Mercury

D/S: 0.38 A.U.
D: 3,032 mi. (4,880 km)
RP: 59 Earth-days
Y: 88 Earth-days
T: −279° to 801°F (−173° to 427°C)
GP: 38 lbs. (17.2 kg)
S: 0

- Eighth largest planet; closest to the sun
- Difficult to see without a telescope
- Surface is hot and dry; features cliffs, craters, and plains
- Thin atmosphere contains helium, hydrogen, oxygen, and sodium and causes the greatest temperature range among the planets

Mars

D/S: 1.52 A.U.
D: 4,222 mi. (6,794 km)
RP: 24 hrs. 37 min.
Y: 686.98 Earth-days
T: −225° to 63F (−143° to 17°C)
GP: 38 lbs. (17.2 kg)
S: 2

- Seventh largest planet; fourth from the sun
- Nicknamed the "Red Planet" because its red rocks and dust give it a reddish glow
- The only planet whose surface can be studied in detail from Earth; features large polar ice caps, gorges, meteor craters, and volcanoes. Some gorges are larger than Earth's Grand Canyon; the largest crater is about 1,242 mi. (2,000 km) wide; the largest volcano is about 2.5 times taller than Earth's Mount Everest.
- Atmosphere is thin and largely consists of carbon dioxide; also contains nitrogen
- Water exists only as a solid or as vapor; it cannot exist on Mars as a liquid.
- Strong seasonal winds cause dust storms—some of which may cover the entire planet.
- The only other planet in the solar system some scientists believe may contain life

Uranus

D/S: 19.22 A.U.
D: 31,760 mi. (51,118 km)
RP: 17 hrs. 8 min.
Y: 30,685 Earth-days
T: −357°F (−216°C)
GP: n/a
S: 27

- Third largest planet; seventh from the sun
- It was often disregarded as a star before the invention of the telescope.
- Unlike other planets, its rotation is nearly parallel with its orbit around the sun.
- Atmosphere is 83% hydrogen, 15% helium, and 2% methane.
- May have a small, rocky core
- Features 11 thin, faint rings of orbiting rock and/or ice

Venus

D/S: 0.7 A.U.
D: 7,521 mi. (12,103 km)
RP: 243 Earth-days
Y: 224.7 Earth-days
T: 864°F (462°C)
GP: 88 lbs. (39.9 kg)
S: 0

- Sixth largest planet; second from the sun
- Called "Earth's twin" because the two planets are similar in size
- When viewed from Earth, appears brighter than all stars but the sun; as Venus travels toward Earth in its orbit, it appears as an "evening star" and as it travels away, it appears as a "morning star."
- Hot, dry surface of canyons, mountains, plains, and valleys is surrounded by a thick cloud of sulfuric acid. Thousands of volcanoes are present.
- Atmosphere is mainly carbon dioxide. There are several layers of very thick clouds of sulfuric acid. Atmospheric pressure is 90 times greater than Earth's, making it the heaviest of all the planets. Winds in the upper atmosphere exceed speeds of 186 mph (300 kmph).
- Rotation is opposite that of the other planets

Jupiter

D/S: 5.2 A.U.
D: 88,850 mi. (142,984 km)
RP: 9 hrs. 55 min.
Y: 4,332.7 Earth-days
T: −250°F (−157°C)
GP: 253 lbs. (115 kg)
S: 63

- Largest planet; fifth from the sun
- While its mass is more than two times greater than all the other planets combined, its density is only slightly greater than water.
- Fastest spinning planet
- Basically liquid—90% hydrogen and 10% helium—possible core of rocky material
- The "Great Red Spot" is a high-pressure storm system twice the size of Earth; observed for over 300 years.
- Its intense internal heat causes it to give off almost twice as much energy as it gets from the sun
- Its four largest satellites—Callisto, Europa, Ganymede, and Io—were discovered by Galileo, an Italian astronomer, in 1610 and are called the Galilean moons.
- Orbiting dust particles create a faint, thin ring.

Neptune

D/S: 30.09 A.U.
D: 30,775 mi. (49,528 km)
RP: 16 hrs. 7 min.
Y: 60,190 Earth-days
T: −353°F (−214°C)
GP: n/a
S: 13

- Fourth largest planet; eighth from the sun
- Cannot be seen from Earth without a telescope
- Every 248 years—for a 20-year period—its orbit moves outside that of Pluto's, making it the most distant planet in the solar system.
- Atmosphere is mainly hydrogen and helium; bluish color caused by clouds of methane.
- May have a small, rocky core
- Releases more than twice as much energy as it receives from the sun
- Has several dark rings; composition unknown

Earth

D/S: 1 A.U.
D: 7,926 mi. (12,756 km)
RP: 23 hrs. 56 min.
T: −128.6° to 136°F (−89.6° to 58°C)
GP: 100 lbs. (45 kg)
S: 1

- Fifth largest planet; third from the sun
- At least 4.5 billion years old
- Only planet known to support life
- The surface consists of about 70% water and 30% land.
- Features deep oceans, large polar ice caps, mountains, low valleys, and volcanoes
- Atmosphere is about 78% nitrogen, 21% oxygen, and 1% argon and other gases; also contains water vapor and dust

Saturn

D/S: 9.55 A.U.
D: 74,900 mi. (120,536 km)
RP: 10 hrs. 39 min.
Y: 10,759 Earth-days
T: −288°F (−178°C)
GP: 107 lbs. (48.5 kg)
S: 34+

- Second largest planet; sixth from the sun
- Though it has the second greatest mass, it is less dense than water.
- Atmosphere is 75% hydrogen and 25% helium—mainly layers of liquid hydrogen; may have a rocky core
- Winds of up to 1,118 mph (1,800 kmph) cause such turbulent storms as the "Great White Spot," which may surround the planet.
- Intense interior radiates 2.5 times more energy than it receives from the sun.
- Rocks, dust, and ice orbiting the planet form several large rings and thousands of narrow ringlets about 6 mi. (10 km) thick.
- Its largest satellite, Titan, has an atmosphere.
- Can be observed from Earth with the naked eye; rings require a telescope

Pluto

D/S: 39.51 A.U.
D: 1,454 mi. (2,340 km)
RP: 6 Earth-days
Y: 90,800 Earth-days
T: −387 to −369°F (−233 to −223°C)
GP: n/a
S: 3

- Smallest in size and mass; farthest from the sun
- Cannot be viewed from Earth without a telescope
- Little is known about its surface; may be 70% rock and 30% water ice much like the moon Triton; atmosphere of nitrogen, carbon monoxide, and methane
- Highly elliptical orbit: every 248 years—for a 20-year period—its orbit moves inside Neptune's; some scientists suggest Pluto may be an escaped moon, possibly from Neptune's orbit.
- Like Uranus, its equator is almost at right angles to its orbit.

D/S	=	Average Distance from Sun
D	=	Diameter
RP	=	Rotation Period
Y	=	Length of Year
T	=	Temperature
GP	=	Gravitational Pull
S	=	Number of Satellites

Stars

- Glowing balls of hot gases—usually hydrogen and helium
- Vary in size, color, and magnitude, or brightness
- Classified as O, B, A, F, G, K, or M:
  O—blue giant; very bright, very hot; about 63,000°F (35,000°C)
  B—blue-white; about 36,000°F (20,000°C)
  A—white; about 18,000°F (10,000°C)
  F—yellow-white; about 13,500°F (7,500°C)
  G—yellow; about 10,800°F (6,000°C)
  K—orange; about 8,460°F (4,700°C)
  M—red dwarf; about 5,400°F (3,000°C)
- Additional star-related terms:

Binary: Pair of stars that revolve around each other but appear as one object when seen with the naked eye; often alter in brightness when eclipsing each other if one star is brighter than the other; may be close enough to touch or millions of miles or kilometers apart

Black hole: Collapsed object, such as a star, that becomes invisible because its gravitational pull is so strong that not even light can escape

Globular cluster: a group of stars smaller than a galaxy

Neutron star: A small, extremely dense star composed of tightly packed neutrons; results from a supernova

Pulsar: A neutron star that regularly gives off bursts of radio waves

Red giant: A star that has swelled to become as much as a hundred times larger than Earth's sun; appears red because it is cooler than most stars

Betelgeuse (Alpha Orionis) a red supergiant in the constellation Orion

Globular Cluster G1/Mayall II

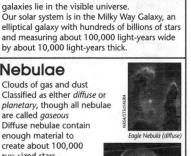
Black hole in Galaxy NGC 7052

Sun (sunspots present)

Supernova 1987A

Supergiant: A large star thousands of times brighter than Earth's sun

Sun: Star in Earth's solar system; It is about 863,710 mi. (1,390,000 km) in diameter and consists of about 70% hydrogen and about 28% helium. At about 4.5 billion years old, it is about half way through its life.

Sunspot: A dark region on the sun's surface; Sunspots are cooler than other areas on the sun's surface, shine less brightly, and appear dark.

Supernova: A star that explodes, becomes billions of times brighter than usual for a few weeks, and results in a black hole or a neutron star

Galaxies

- Gas, dust, and stars—a few billion to more than a trillion—held together by gravity
- Range in size from a few thousand to half a million light-years in diameter
- Shape may be spiral, elliptical, or irregular
- May lie alone or cluster in groups of a few dozen to several thousand
- An estimated 100 billion galaxies lie in the visible universe.
- Our solar system is in the Milky Way Galaxy, an elliptical galaxy with hundreds of billions of stars and measuring about 100,000 light-years wide by about 10,000 light-years thick.

M100 (spiral galaxy)

NGC 4881 (elliptical galaxy)

Nebulae

- Clouds of gas and dust
- Classified as either *diffuse* or *planetary*, though all nebulae are called *gaseous*
- Diffuse nebulae contain enough material to create about 100,000 sun-sized stars.
- Planetary nebulae around a collapsing star may form from the star's outer atmospheric layer.

Eagle Nebula (diffuse)

Cat's Eye Nebula (planetary)

Moon

- A natural satellite that orbits a planet
- All but two of the planets have moons.
- Earth's moon is about 4.6 billion years old. As it orbits the earth, sunlight reflects off the moon and gives it various appearances, called *phases* (see below). The moon lies about 238,857 mi. (384,403 km) from earth and has a diameter of 2,160 mi. (3,476 km). Its rotation period is 27 days, 7 hours, 43 minutes. Its surface is mainly rock and soil, but no water. It has little or no atmosphere.

new moon | waxing crescent | first quarter | waxing gibbous | full moon | waning gibbous | last quarter | waning crescent

Constellations

- Eighty-eight regions in the sky—named for animals, heroes and heroines, mythical creatures, and scientific instruments—that represent particular groups of visible stars
- As the earth orbits the sun, different constellations become visible in the night sky.

Orion

Asteroids & Meteoroids

- Asteroids are crater-covered rocks that orbit the sun, mainly in the "asteroid belt" between Mars and Jupiter.
- Meteoroids are asteroids caught by Earth's gravity.
- Asteroids measure from 635 mi. (1,023 km) to 1 in. (2.5 cm) or smaller.
- A meteoroid that burns up in the atmosphere is called a meteor, or "shooting star."
- A meteoroid that falls to Earth without burning up is called a meteorite; at impact, it may leave a crater.

Asteroid Vesta

Meteorite fragment from Vesta

Additional Terms

Astronomical unit (AU): The average distance between the earth and the sun—about 93 million mi. (150 million km); often used to measure distances within the solar system

Atmosphere: Gases held by gravity around an object in space

Aurora: Nighttime, colored light display called *aurora borealis* or Northern Lights in the Northern Hemisphere, and *aurora australis* or Southern lights in the Southern Hemisphere; forms arcs, bands, curtains, or rays and may appear to brighten, flicker, or wave; usually green, but also blue, purple, or red; caused by solar particles caught by a planet's magnetic field

Axis: An imaginary straight line around which a celestial body rotates; Earth's axis runs from the North Pole to the South Pole.

Corona: Outer edge of the sun's atmosphere; usually studied during a solar eclipse

Eclipse, lunar: Partial or complete blocking of the moon as viewed from Earth; caused when the Earth aligns between the sun and the moon

Eclipse, solar: A partial or complete blocking of the sun as viewed from Earth; caused when the moon aligns between Earth and the sun

Gravity: The force exerted by a celestial body that pulls objects toward it

Light-year: The distance light travels in a year at a speed of 186,282 mi. (299,792 km) per second: 5.88 trillion mi. (9.46 trillion km); used to measure distances outside the solar system

Mass: The amount of matter in an object

Orbit: The path of one object around another; For example, the moon travels around the Earth and the path the moon takes is its orbit.

Satellite: An object that continuously orbits another; an *artificial satellite* is created on Earth and launched into space to orbit a planet, moon, etc. for communication and/or research purposes; a *natural satellite* is an object in space, such as the Earth's moon, that orbits another object in space.

Solar flare: A sudden eruption of hydrogen from the sun; temperatures in a solar flare are much hotter than on the sun's surface.

Solar radiation: Energy emitted from the sun in the form of heat; light; plasma; gamma, infrared, ultraviolet and X-rays; and radio waves

Solar system: A star and the objects that travel around it; includes planets, satellites, comets, asteroids, and meteoroids and is usually disk-shaped

Telescope, optical: A tool used to study distant objects in space

Universe: All matter and energy in space

Weight: The force on an object caused by the pull of gravity

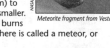
Solar eclipse

Comet

- "Dirty snowball" of water, ice, and dust that orbits the sun
- Features a nucleus (center), a coma (head), and a tail that always faces away from the sun
- A head and a tail form when the ice is heated by the sun, melts, and is given off as a dust-filled gas.
- Particles in the tail may cause a meteor shower on Earth if the planet passes through the tail.
- Famous comets include Hale-Bopp, Halley, Hyakutake, and Shoemaker-Levy 9.

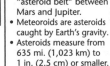
Hale-Bopp

Periodic Table of the Elements

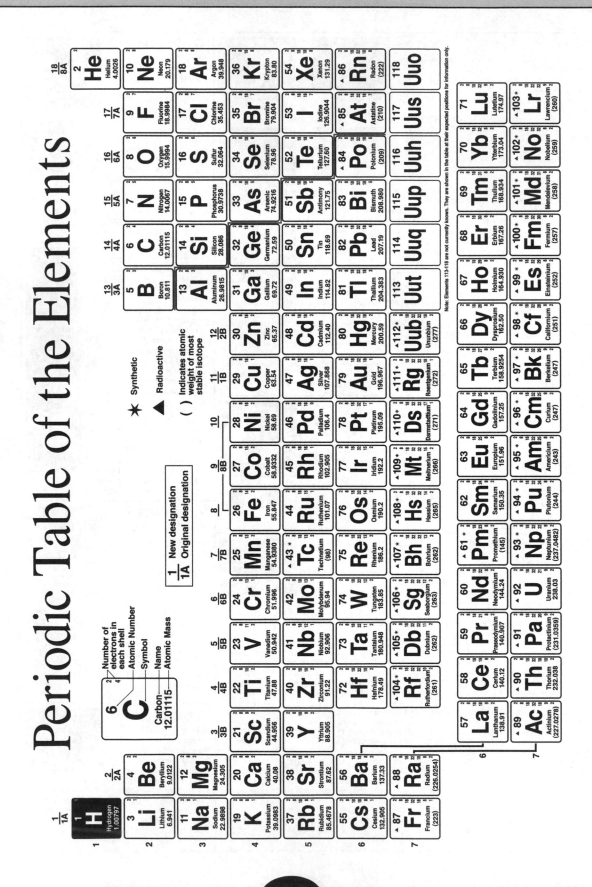

Science Fair Basics

The **scientific method** is the way scientists learn and study the world around them. You become a scientist when you try to find answers to your questions by using the scientific method.

Asking questions and coming up with answers is the basis for the scientific method. So, when you begin your science project, you begin with a question that you have. The educated guess you make about this question is called a **hypothesis**.

After you have asked the question and made an educated guess, you have to perform tests to determine whether or not your hypothesis is right. To test your hypothesis, you must follow a **procedure**, which is the name given to the steps you take in your experiment or fieldwork. Your experiment or fieldwork should give you information that can be measured. For instance, if you are trying to determine whether bears are happier in the wild or in the zoo, you must decide how you are going to measure happiness. Perhaps you base the bear's happiness on the amount of food it eats. Putting your information in measurable terms allows you to show **quantitatively** (through numbers) whether your hypothesis is correct or incorrect. It is also important to conduct your test multiple times and use as many test subjects as possible to make sure your results are consistent before you make your conclusion.

Your **conclusion** describes how your **data**, or the results you received from your experiment, compare to your hypothesis. Did your data show that you were right in your educated guess, or did it show that you were wrong? A disproved hypothesis is just as important as a proven hypothesis because it gave important information to others. Your conclusion should also include any new questions that arise as you are doing your experiment. Perhaps when testing whether a bear is happier in the wild or in the zoo, you find that you are not seeing a change in the bear's eating habits, but you do notice that they act differently towards other bears. Your new question might be, how does a bear's interaction with other bears change in different environments? What might seem like a failed hypothesis may turn into a new question and an even better experiment.

The Birth of the Scientific Method

*Galileo Galilei (1564–1642), an Italian astronomer and physicist, believed in discovering facts by first forming a theory (or hypothesis) and then testing it in an experiment, just as you do in your science project. This approach, which we call the **scientific method**, was a very radical idea in his time. People were more inclined to accept ideas that were in line with their religious beliefs or, that seemed logical. But many scientific discoveries do not always appear to make sense. For instance, many of Galileo's contemporaries did not believe that other planets had satellites (like our moon) because they could not see them with their own eyes. Galileo was willing to explore these questions that others had dismissed. He also believed in careful observation and measurement and developed the telescope into a powerful tool for exploring the sky. With this tool he discovered four of Jupiter's satellites. Galileo's desire to test his theories through experiment and learn through observation and measurement moved science forward.*

The Scientific Method

The scientific method is the backbone of your science fair project. The scientific method has four parts:

Observation

You notice something in the world that you want to know more about, so you ask a question. The purpose of your science fair project is to answer this question.

Hypothesis

You **predict** why, when, where, or how whatever you observed happened, based on information you already have. Sometimes this takes the form of an "if . . . then" statement. A hypothesis is often called an "educated guess" because you base your prediction on facts you already know.

Testing

Test your hypothesis with a procedure. You can do either an experiment, where everything except the particular thing being tested is carefully controlled, or fieldwork, where you study your subject in the natural world. Careful observations and measurements are recorded in both testing procedures.

Conclusion

You state whether or not your hypothesis was correct based on the results of your testing. If your hypothesis is proven wrong, try to explain why. Make any further predictions your results could point to, and describe any changes to your procedure you think would give more accurate results or be helpful to further research. Also include any questions you may have thought of during your testing.

Procedure

Procedure is the name given to the steps you take to test your hypothesis.

The purpose of science is to discover things about the world, with accuracy, truth, and objectivity. Scientists:

- test ideas.

- weigh evidence carefully.

- come to conclusions cautiously.

- make conclusions based on facts.

An important part of the scientist's process of discovery is the procedure. A procedure is a list of steps. The steps you plan to take to test your hypothesis must be clearly written out so that someone else could repeat what you have done. Your procedure:

- gives step-by-step directions on what to do.

- lists all the materials and equipment you use.

- provides any instructions you need to build or use equipment.

Experiment and Fieldwork

Scientists test their hypotheses either through experiment or fieldwork.

Experiment

Experimental observations are made in a controlled **environment** that you create. How do you create a controlled environment? You isolate what it is you are investigating in the real world and scale it down so that it is smaller and more simplified.

In an experiment, a scientist tries to look at how just one thing affects a subject. The tricky part is creating an environment in which only that one thing changes. That is why you often see scientists using test tubes, petri dishes, and other small, enclosed settings for their experiment. It is easier to control what occurs in such environments.

Fieldwork

In fieldwork, a scientist goes into an uncontrolled environment and records his or her observations. What is complicated about fieldwork is that while you are recording your observations, you must make sure that you yourself are not interfering with your subject simply by being there. For instance, you cannot count birds in a tree if you scare any away while you try to count them.

Field Study Finds New Life-Forms

Your field study may occur in your own backyard or even at the local nature preserve, but can you imagine exploring the deep rifts in the ocean's floor in a submarine?

In 1977, scientists aboard the research submarine Alvin, from Woods Hole Oceanographic Institute, discovered a new ecosystem, or community of organisms, thriving near volcanic vents at the bottom of the freezing waters of the Pacific Ocean's Galapagos Rift.

The high heat and hydrogen sulfide from the cracks in the volcanoes provide the energy for special bacteria, a staple of the unique food chain there. Other members of the ecosystem are huge tube worms that measure up to 25 feet long. Because they are so different than anything else known by scientists, they are classified in a phylum, Vestimentifera, by themselves. The scientists named some of the new worms alvinellid worms, after their submarine research vessel.

This strange volcanic ecosystem, based on converting sulphurous chemicals into food, suggests to some scientists the possibility that there may be similar strange life-forms on other planets with volcanic activity.

Variables, Controls, Groups, and Trials

When you want to prove a theory true or false, create an experiment that will test one thing you can observe. If you set up a controlled situation and purposely change only one thing, this alteration will cause something else to happen. The thing you purposely change is called the **changing variable**. If your change causes something else to happen, this "something else" is called the **responding variable**, because it is responding to the change.

You must plan your procedure carefully to be sure that you change only one thing in your **experimental group**.

> *Suppose you want to know what would happen if you played music for an experimental group of plants. You will play music, your changing variable, and watch for any signs of a responding variable, which you expect to be bigger or faster growth.*

But how will you know if any growth is a change? How will you know what is bigger and faster growth? You need a way to compare the rate of growth. You need to have something to compare your experimental plants to—something to show what normal growth is. So you need a **control group**. In this experiment, you need to create a control group by raising some other plants in exactly the same way that you raise your experimental group, except that they will not experience the changing variable. You will treat them exactly the same way you do the experimental group, but you will not play music for them.

Your experimental group—Give these plants x amount of food, y amount of water, and play music for them.

Your control group—Use the same kind and age and size of plants, give them the same amounts of food and water, but do not expose them to any music.

You can measure the growth of the plants that you expose to music against the growth of the plants that you don't.

You still need to consider some other things. Can you think of anything else that could affect the plants? How about diseases or pests? Could some of the plants have been healthier than others before you even started the experiment? That is possible, even though you looked them over carefully before you began.

To ensure that any recorded change is from your changing variable, and only from your changing variable, you should test in groups of at least 25 subjects.

For example, if you only tested one or two plants and they both died, you could not be sure that their death resulted from your experiment, or if they were weak before being part of the experiment and were about to die anyway. But if you tested a group of 25 subjects and only two died, you could more confidently conclude that those two plants had been weak or ill before the experiment began.

To be reasonably sure that nothing happens randomly (by chance), you also should run at least three **trials**—do your experiment three times. For example, if you ran your experiment once and correctly used a group of at least 25 subjects, but they all died, you could not be sure their death was the result of your experiment. Perhaps they had all been weak or ill before they were affected by your experiment. If you have at least three trials, and the results are similar each time, you can feel more confident that your results are accurate. If one of the trials gives results that are inconsistent with the others, you can suspect a problem with the odd trial.

Let's See!

On the next page, you will find examples of variables and control groups. In Table 1, take the subject and apply the changing variable to it to see if there would be a change in the responding variable. Table 2 adds a control group that does not experience the changing variable.

If change takes place in the experimental group but not in the control group, you can be reasonably sure your changing variable caused the alteration in the responding variable.

If change occurs in both the experimental and control groups, something else, other than your changing variable, caused the alteration in the responding variable.

Here are three hypotheses to test:

- If I add alcohol to water, the freezing time will change.

- If I give plants plant food, the rate of growth will change.

- If I add color to potatoes, the taste will change.

Here are variables to test the hypotheses in three different experiments:

Table 1 Variables

Subject	Changing Variables	Responding Variables
WATER	ALCOHOL	THE FREEZING TIME
PLANTS	PLANT FOOD	THE RATE OF GROWTH
POTATO	COLOR	THE TASTE OF THE POTATO

Here are experimental and control groups to test in the three different experiments:

Table 2 Experimental & Control Groups

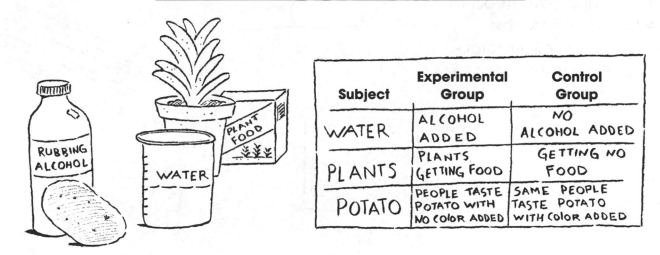

Subject	Experimental Group	Control Group
WATER	ALCOHOL ADDED	NO ALCOHOL ADDED
PLANTS	PLANTS GETTING FOOD	GETTING NO FOOD
POTATO	PEOPLE TASTE POTATO WITH NO COLOR ADDED	SAME PEOPLE TASTE POTATO WITH COLOR ADDED

Observations and Measurements

Every time you look at something, listen to something, or feel something, you are actually measuring it. Some of our most important inventions—for example the microscope, telescope, and thermometer, measure things. You can measure things with scales, thermometers, barometers, microscopes, telescopes, spectroscopes, and geiger counters.

MICROSCOPE

It is very important that your measurements and the words you use to describe your measurements are exact. What is the difference between "less than a liter" and "almost a liter"? If you tell someone to turn "a little way" down the road, couldn't they make a wrong turn and get lost? In order to get accurate results in science, you need to be exact when you measure and when you describe things. That way, other scientists can follow your procedure and get the same results.

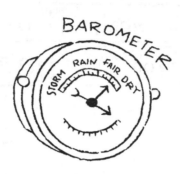
BAROMETER

SPECTROSCOPE

TELESCOPE

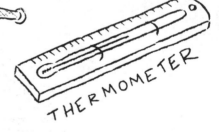
THERMOMETER

AMPLIFIER

GEIGER COUNTER

Qualitative and Quantitative Measurements

There are two ways to observe things: qualitatively and quantitatively. **Qualitative data** describes the quality, or characteristic, of something. If something grows, boils, freezes, burns, tastes sour, changes color, dries out, smells, moves, makes noise, or changes in any way from its original state, you want to make note of that. You should describe shapes, colors, smells, sounds, activity, and any other characteristics you observe.

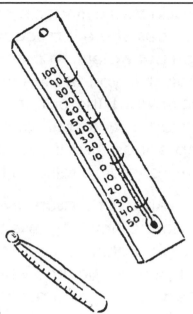

Usually you can find out more about what is happening, and then describe it in greater detail by measuring it with a standard measuring tool such as a ruler or scale. The data you acquire is **quantitative data**.

When you want to describe a qualitative measurement more precisely, you make a quantitative measurement. You may have described a sample as "very cold." But if you want a more precise description, you'll want to measure the temperature of your sample with a thermometer.

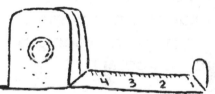

The most important thing in quantitative measurement is knowing how to use the measuring tool you've chosen. When you measure the length of something with a ruler, you cannot say you know exactly how long something is but only that you know the length plus or minus the smallest part marked on the ruler. That is because you are only guessing the distance between the smallest markings. If the smallest lines are millimeters, then your measurement is plus or minus 1 millimeter. When you stand on a scale in the bathroom, it usually only marks the pounds, and so you estimate the partial pounds, the area indicated between the lines. The scale measurement is plus or minus 1 pound.

When you are measuring liquids, you may be using a graduated cylinder, measuring cups, eyedroppers, or other devices. There is a special trick to measuring liquids. When you put water in a measuring cup and hold it at eye level to look at it, you will see that the surface of the water curves downward. The bottom of the curve in a column of water is called a **meniscus**, and you want to measure that, not the top edges. Also, if you use an eyedropper, be careful to let only one drop fall at a time.

Always measure everything you can. Whenever you describe anything, use measurements. Note the length, weight, volume, area, temperature, age, number of things, and the time when things occur. Use the same measuring tool to measure all of the items in a group. So that there is no difference in measurement due to differently marked tools, called **calibrated tools**. When measuring the length or volume of things that may expand when heated, measure them all at the same temperature. Record both the temperature and the measurement.

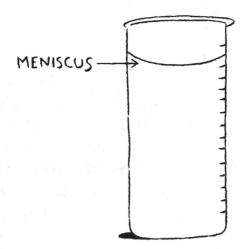

MENISCUS →

Here are some handy measuring tools you can find around the house:

TO MEASURE LENGTH

- measuring tape
- ruler
- yardstick
- meter stick

TO MEASURE WEIGHT

- postage scale
- bathroom scale
- food scale

TO MEASURE VOLUME

- measuring spoons
- eyedropper
- measuring cups
- pint, quart, gallon milk cartons
- liter soft drink bottles

TO MEASURE TEMPERATURE

- body temperature thermometer
- indoor/outdoor air temperature thermometer
- candy or cooking thermometer

TO MEASURE AIR PRESSURE

- barometer
- tire pressure gauge

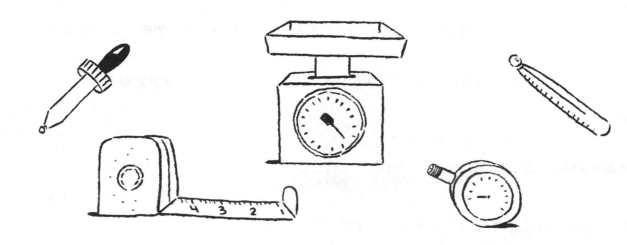

Timetable

Use this timetable as a model to plan the organization of your science fair project. You must understand before you start how much time it will take to do the things you plan to do, such as develop film, grow plants or seeds, or watch animals develop. You must leave time to change things or even start over, if necessary. This timetable gives you four months, but you can add to that if you want to start earlier and spend more time on some things. Remember that most of your work will have to be done on weekends and after school.

Week 1
❏   Follow the questions in this book to choose your topic.

Week 2 – 4
❏   Go to the library and contact experts to research your topic.

❏   Create your bibliography.

Week 5 – 7
❏   Plan your project. Fill out and get forms OK'd to use tissue samples or animal or human subjects, if that is allowed at your fair.

❏   Collect the materials you will need to do your project.

Week 8 – 10
❏   Start your notebook and run your experiment or do your fieldwork. If you are using photography, develop the film.

Week 11 – 13
❏   Continue your experiment or fieldwork. Redo your experiment or fieldwork, if necessary.

❏   If you have time, begin writing your report and building your display.

Week 14 – 16
❏   Write and proofread your report.

❏   Get supplies to create your display and put together your exhibit.

Week 17
❏   Set up your exhibit and enjoy the science fair!

Safety

Safety is a consideration of the utmost importance when you are planning a science project. Follow these tips to protect yourself and others:

- Always have a teacher, parent, or other responsible adult supervise you, unless after you have explained exactly what you are going to do, and the adult gives you permission to work on your own.

- Pay attention and be alert while you are doing your experiment. Fooling around can be very dangerous.

- Wear protective goggles, thick gloves, and a lab apron whenever you work with dangerous materials or chemicals. Move or tie up any loose clothing or hair. Work on a protected surface and organize your materials so that they are within your reach. Put away anything you do not need, and keep your work area neat.

- If you are doing fieldwork outdoors, dress appropriately, with protective boots, long pants, sunglasses, and sunscreen, if needed. Avoid any poisonous plants and threatening animals.

- If you are using any dangerous materials or chemicals, read all the labels before beginning your experiment.

- Do not inhale fumes produced in any chemical reactions. Do not taste chemicals or solutions.

- Do not eat or drink anything while you are doing your experiment. Clean your hands carefully after you finish working.

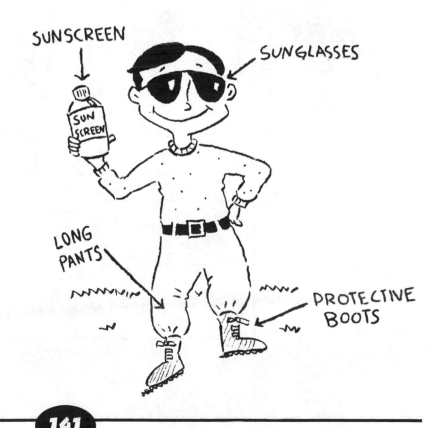

SUNSCREEN

SUNGLASSES

LONG PANTS

PROTECTIVE BOOTS

- Watch out for sharp edges, and be careful handling glass objects. Do not touch glass that has been recently heated.

- Never tinker with household electricity or power or gas lines. Do not touch any high-voltage source or anything connected to one. Never put an electrical device in water.

- Keep a first aid kit nearby, as well as a fire extinguisher and a bucket of water for putting out possible fires. Have hand mitts ready to protect your hands. Do not put water on an oil-based fire, because the water could actually spread the fire. Instead, smother that kind of fire with baking soda or a blanket.

- Do not reach over open flames or heating instruments.

- Be sure you have plenty of time to run your experiment safely. You should never have to rush.

Glossary

acid: an electrolyte that increases the concentration of hydrogen in a substance
air pressure: the force of the weight of air on everything else on earth
astronomy: the study of the universe
atom: a tiny particle made of protons, neutrons, and electrons
ball-and-socket joint: joint that makes a swinging, rotating movement, like your wrist
base: an electrolyte that increases the concentration of hydroxide in a substance
broad leaves: trees that have leaves of all different shapes and sizes
camouflage: coloring that lets animals blend in to their surroundings
cartilage: soft bone that make up your nose, ears, and pads between backbones
catalyst: controls the rate of a chemical reaction
chlorophyll: green material in plants used to make food
chromosomes: the thread-like parts of cells that hold genes
circuit: a path along which electricity travels
circulatory system: the system made up of the heart, arteries, veins, and capillaries
clouds: water droplets collected on tiny specks of dust or salt particles in the air
compound machine: a machine made of two or more simple machines
conclusion: a summary of the procedure and results of an experiment
conduction: movement of heat through a solid material, transferring energy
conductor: a substance that carries electricity, such as metal
conifers: trees with needle-like leaves
consumer: animals that cannot make their own food and have to get it from other plants or animals
convection: movement of heated material from one place to another, transferring energy
conventional system: system of measurement used in the U.S., including feet, gallons, and pounds
density: measures how much mass fills a given amount of space
desalination: removing salt and other minerals from ocean water
dicot: a plant that has bundles of food tubes throughout the stem
digestive system: system that breaks down food collecting nutrients and getting rid of wastes
ecosystem: a group of plants and animals interacting and living in the same community
endangered: animals that are in danger of becoming extinct
endocrine system: the system that develops and releases hormones into the blood
energy: the ability to do work
erosion: process of moving surface soil with wind, water, ice, or gravity
extinct: animals that are gone forever
fixed joint: a joint that does not move
food chain: group of plants and animals that feed off one another
food web: a series of interconnected food chains
force: the push or pull that one object exerts on another
friction: the force that keeps some things from moving or slows them down when they do move
genes: parts of the cell that determine characteristic living things inherit from their parents
geologic time scale: system used to divide earth's history into meaningful parts
gliding joint: several bones next to one another bend together in limited gliding motion
gravity: a force that draws objects toward itself
hibernation: a long, heavy sleep that lasts all winter for some animals
hinge joint: joint that moves in only one direction like a door hinge
humidity: amount of moisture in the air
hydrosphere: all the water that exists on earth
igneous rock: rocks that come from the magma of volcanic eruptions
insulator: a substance that does not carry electricity, such as rubber

Glossary

integumentary system: the system made up of hair, skin, and nails

invertebrates: animals that do not have a backbone

landforms: features of the landscape, such as mountains, plains, plateaus, and deltas

lunar eclipse: when the Sun, Earth, and Moon are in a direct line and the Moon moves into the Earth's shadow

magnetism: the push and pull force of a magnet

marrow: substance inside bones

matter: anything that occupies space and has mass

metamorphic rocks: rocks that are formed from other kinds of rocks through pressure and heat under the earth

metric system: system of measurement used around the world, including grams, liters, and meters

minerals: solid substances found in nature

Mohs Hardness Scale: classifies a mineral's hardness using a simple scratch test

monocot: a plant that has bundles of food tubes arranged in a ring around the edge of the stem

muscular system: the system of muscles that allow the body to move and hold the body together

nervous system: the system made up of the brain and spinal cord that send information through the body

Newton's Laws of Motion: objects at rest stay at rest and objects in motion stay in motion; acceleration of an object depends on its mass and the size and direction of the force acting on it; every action has an equal and opposite reaction force

photosynthesis: process of plants getting energy from sunlight

pivot joint: a joint that makes a rotating motion

prediction: what you think will happen in an experiment, based on what you know about the relationship of the things you are testing

procedure: steps done in an experiment

producers: plants that use photosynthesis to make their own food

pulse: the feeling of blood pumped through veins by the heart

purpose: reason for doing an experiment; what you want to learn from the experiment

radiation: a special type of wave that delivers heat and light, transferring energy

reproductive system: the system that allows living things to create new life

respiratory system: the system made up of the lungs that takes in oxygen and pushes out carbon dioxide

results: outcome of each procedure in an experiment

sedimentary rocks: rocks that are formed from hardened layers of sediment eroded off older rocks

simple machine: something that changes the direction of the force or the amount of force requires to move an object

skeletal system: the system of bones in a body

soil: a mixture of rock particles, and decaying vegetable and animal matter

solar eclipse: when the new Moon is between the Earth and the Sun blocking the view of the Sun

solar system: system made up of the Sun and the nine planets and their moons that orbit it

state of matter: the form matter takes, either solid, liquid, or gas

tectonic plates: plates that move beneath the earth's surface, causing earthquakes, eruptions, and continental movement

temperature: the heat or coolness of the air around us

tsunami: a seismic sea wave caused by tectonic plate movement

urinary system: system made up of the kidneys and bladder that rids the body of waste

vertebrates: animals that have a backbone

water cycle: process of water moving from one place to another in the hydrosphere